JOSHUA

Dale Ralph Davis

JOSHUA

No Falling Words

Dale Ralph Davis

CHRISTIAN
FOCUS

Dale Ralph Davis is pastor of Woodlands Presbyterian Church, Hattiesburg, Mississippi. Previously he taught Old Testament at Reformed Theological Seminary, Jackson, Mississippi. He has previously written commentaries on *Judges* (978-1-84550-138-9), *1 Samuel* (978-1-85792-516-6), *2 Samuel* (978-1-84550-270-6), *1 Kings* (978-1-84550-251-5) and *2 Kings* (978-1-84550-096-2).

Copyright © Dale Ralph Davis

ISBN 978-1-84550-137-2

10 9 8 7 6 5 4 3 2 1

This edition published in 2000,
reprinted in 2003, 2006, 2008 & 2010
by
Christian Focus Publications Ltd.,
Geanies House, Fearn, Ross-shire,
IV20 1TW, Scotland, UK.

www.christianfocus.com

Previously published in 1988 and 1996 by
Baker Book House, Grand Rapids, USA

Cover design by Alister MacInnes

Printed and bound by
Bell & Bain, Glasgow

Mixed Sources
Product group from well-managed forests and other controlled sources
www.fsc.org Cert no.TT-COC-002769
© 1996 Forest Stewardship Council

Contents

Abbreviations

ASV	American Standard Version
IBD	*Illustrated Bible Dictionary*
ISBE	*International Standard Bible Encyclopedia*
IDB	*Interpreter's Dictionary of the Bible*
IDB/S	*Interpreter's Dictionary of the Bible/Supplementary Volume*
JB	Jerusalem Bible
NASB	New American Standard Bible
NEB	New English Bible
NIV	New International Version
NJB	New Jerusalem Bible
RSV	Revised Standard Version
TDOT	*Theological Dictionary of the Old Testament*
TEV	Today's English Version
TWOT	*Theological Wordbook of the Old Testament*
ZPEB	*Zondervan Pictorial Encyclopedia of the Bible*

Preface

I remember learning one rule in Speech 101 in college: never begin a speech with an apology. Since this is not a speech but is a book, I will break the rule – at least with some disclaimers.

This commentary is obviously not a critical, linguistic, grammatical, archaeological thesaurus on Joshua. There is a reason for that: I neither can nor want to write that sort of commentary. Certainly, you will find grammatical details or critical discussions – at least bits and pieces of them – in this study. But the focus is necessarily elsewhere. I do not know multiple Near Eastern languages (such as Ugaritic or Akkadian) and so cannot stress linguistics; I am not a trained archaeologist or historian and so do not emphasize backgrounds; and I am skeptical of the usefulness of cerebral critical positions, which frequently seem intent on considering everything but the text as it stands, and so will not enter barren disputes. My purpose has been to provide a model of what a pastor can do in biblical study if he will sweat over the Hebrew text and assume that the text as we have it was meant to be bread from God for his people. My conviction is that if one is willing to keep his Hebrew Bible before his eyes, a congregation of God's people next to his heart, and the struggle of hermenueutics (i.e. what does this writer intend to proclaim to God's people in his time, and how do I faithfully hold on to that intention and helpfully apply that text to God's contemporary flock?) in his mind, he will have manna to set before God's hungering people.

Clearly, I think commentaries should be written from this conviction and after this pattern. I do not think I can expect my seminary students to *warm* to the Old Testament unless they sense it *nurturing* them as they hear it taught. (Why should not the Spirit be at work in our classrooms?) But if once they feel the *fire* of the Old Testament text – well, then, the Old Testament becomes a new book to them! Certainly, all the technical matters (linguistic, archaeological, critical) are in order; but we must bring the fragments together in an expository treatment that is not ashamed to stoop to the level of application.

In recent years, evangelicals have made much of the inspiration, infallibility and inerrancy of Scripture. Rightly so. But three 'i's' are not enough. We must push the 'instructability' of Scripture. The apostle was surely completely sober when he wrote that the Old Testament is 'profitable' (2 Tim. 3:16). We must demonstrate that. If the church is to recover the Old Testament, our expositions of it must show that, without torturing or twisting, it speaks for the comfort and correction of the saints.

I trust *No Falling Words* approximates such standards. The title comes from Joshua 21:43-45, the sheet anchor of the book (precisely, from verse 45; see also 23:14). There were no falling words among the ancient Genesis promises; no *falling* words means no *failing* words. I trust readers will find the same – that God's promise contains no falling words, only *standing* ones, upon which we, too, can stand.

A couple of mundane matters should be noted. I assume that the reader will have Bible in hand as he or she uses this book. I have drawn on a number of English translations, but, frequently, the translations are my own.

I owe multiple thanks to students, colleagues ,and former par-ishioners for their stimulation and encouragement. I originally finished this volume on Reformation Day, 1987. It was a 'manse' production, written amid the delights and distresses of pastoral ministry. I don't think that is in any way a deficiency! And I am most grateful to Christian Focus for sending it forth in a new format. The book remains dedicated to Yahweh's gift (Prov. 19:14), Barbara, for two reasons: no other human being so richly deserves it, and she wanted me to dedicate it to her!

Introduction

There is no effort here to provide a full introduction to the Book of Joshua. A proposal about the date and setting of the book will be made later (see introductory comments on Joshua 22, including the footnotes). Critical conclusions should be drawn only after careful exposure to the text itself. However, I believe it is important to answer the question, is Joshua among the prophets?

Don't we usually stick Joshua among the historical books, which is the term we use to designate the books of Joshua through 2 Chronicles in our English Bibles? Jewish tradition was probably closer to the truth when it dubbed Joshua through 2 Kings as former prophets.[1]

But why torture ourselves over terms? What difference does it make whether we look on Joshua as a historical or as a prophetical book? It has to do with the way some people think of history. I used to have theological students (who had just begun to get excited about the Old Testament) tell me, 'I never read or studied the Old Testament very much, because it seemed like it was all *history*.' What did they mean by that? They meant that they had viewed the Old Testament as a mere record of historical facts – and a dry one at that. Some of them never liked history in school, and when the Bible was cast in the same form ... alas!

What happens when one looks at Joshua as primarily prophecy rather than history? What is this difference between

---

[1] In distinction from the latter prophets – Isaiah, Jeremiah, Ezekiel, and the Book of the Twelve (the minor prophets) – 1–2 Samuel and 1–2 Kings were viewed as one book each, so that the former prophets comprised four books: Joshua, Judges, Samuel, and Kings.

former prophets and historical books? To oversimplify, it is like the difference between preaching and a world history book. The 'prophecy of Joshua' means to convict, not merely to inform; to comfort, not simply to enlighten. The Book of Joshua is preaching material beamed to Israel in the form of historical narrative. We need to see clearly that 'history in the O[ld] T[estament] is a declaration from God about God'.[2] But until we begin to think of history that way, we will do well to keep thinking of Joshua as one of the former *prophets*.

As you read and study Joshua, try to keep asking yourself the question: What is the writer *preaching about* when he tells me this story? He is not telling you the story only to inform you (although that is part of it); he has a message to proclaim, a God to press upon you.[3]

Keeping this in mind, let us begin.

---

[2] J. A. Motyer, 'Old Testament History', in The Expositor's Bible Commentary, ed. Frank E. Gaebelein, 12 vols. (Grand Rapids: Zondervan, 1979), 1:154.

[3] I agree with Sidney Greidanus when he asserts that historical texts 'do not merely relate past facts but proclaim these facts in a relevant manner to the church at various stages of redemptive history'. He holds that the 'nature of the historical text can best be described ... as proclamation' (*Sola Scriptura: Problems and Principles in Preaching Historical Texts* [Toronto: Wedge Publishing Foundation, 1970], 212). None of the preceding remarks should be viewed as impugning the importance or reliability of biblical history; they are only an attempt to clarify the true nature of that history.

Part 1

Entering the Land

(Joshua 1–4)

I

The Promise of God
and Four Funerals
(Joshua 1:1-18; 24:29-33)

Several months ago I was reading Edward Eggleston's *The Hoosier Schoolboy* to one of my sons. We'd had the book in our collection for some time but had never read it. Finally, Seth and I tackled it. He was quite taken with it and really became caught up in the story. In fact, he read the last chapter on his own so that he would know all along how 'it finally turned out'. That is not a bad idea – even for a biblical book. Normally, one might expect a writer to raise some of his foremost concerns in his introduction and conclusion. Hence, we propose to look at the very beginning *and* the very end of Joshua first in order to gain a perspective from which to view the whole book.

In the case of Joshua, this means that we find ourselves attending four funerals. Let's attend Moses' funeral first and save the rest for later in our discussion.

The Promise of God and the First Funeral (1:1-18)
Before entering into an exposition of the themes of chapter 1, it will be well to notice how the chapter is put together. The chapter falls into two major sections, both of which follow the same main pattern:

15

Death of Moses, 1a
Yahweh's charge to Joshua, 1b-9
   Yahweh's command to action, 1b-4
      'Cross over...'
      'The land I am giving...'
   Yahweh's encouragement to Joshua, 5-9
      'I will be/am with you' (beginning and end of
      section)
      'Be strong and be bold' (three times in the middle of
      section)
Joshua's charge to Israel, 10-18
   Joshua's command to prepare for action, 10-15
   To people (via officers), 10-11
      'You are going to cross over...'
      'The land Yahweh ... is giving'
   To eastern tribes, 12-15
      '*You* must cross over...'
      'The land Yahweh ... is giving'
   People's encouragement to Joshua, 16-18
      'Yahweh ... be with you'
      'Be strong and bold'

From this sketch at least two emphases emerge: the land is
God's gift and yet there is the command to lay hold of that
gift, and encouragement is given to the leader of God's people.
The encouragement in both cases comes to Joshua, who, as we
shall see, doubtless needed it greatly. This theme carries into
chapters 3–4 (see 3:7; 4:14). Interestingly, chapter 1 is almost
entirely direct speech rather than descriptive narrative; the
writer uses the speeches of others to tell his story. Now for a
more detailed exposition.

The Vitality of Yahweh's Promise (1:1-4)

The first theme the writer underscores is the vitality of
Yahweh's promise. The *content* of the promise has to do with
Yahweh's gift of the land (vv. 2-4, 6, 11, 15). And some land!
As in Genesis 15:18, Deuteronomy 1:7, and 11:24, the eastern
boundary is the Euphrates River. You must get out your Bible
atlas to believe or disbelieve it![1] But what is important to see
is that this is the promise God made long ago to Abraham

and company (Gen. 12:6-7; 13:14-15; 15:7, 18-21; 17:8; 24; 26:3-4; 28:13-14; 35:12; 48:3-4; 50:24). Hence the theological roots of Joshua 1 are sunk deeply into the soil of Genesis 12 and following, and that ancient promise is about to receive its contemporary fulfilment.

However, the *context* of the promise – 'after the death of Moses' (v. 1) – is particularly significant. 'Moses my servant has died,' Yahweh says, 'and now, rise, cross over this Jordan ... into the land which I am giving to them' (v. 2). In order to appreciate this reference to Moses' death, one must remember the pentateuchal tradition of the greatness of Moses. Israel stood within an inch of her covenant death in Exodus 32–34; Moses was the only Israelite in covenant fellowship with Yahweh (this is the implication of Exodus 33:7-11 in context), and, as Israel's mediator, he attached their destiny to his (33:16). Unlike prophets in general, Moses received revelation from Yahweh in the most direct manner (Num. 12:1-8). Indeed, Deuteronomy 34:10-12 (the three verses right before Joshua) makes crystal clear how incomparable Moses was. There was no one like Moses; no one as great as Moses until the One greater than Moses came. And now Moses had died. You can imagine the dismay in Israel. Although you expected it, were informed of it, were prepared for it (Deut. 31), what do you do when *the* servant of God dies and a raging river lies between you and the land you are to inherit? (You might wonder if Moses died after all – he is mentioned eleven times in Joshua 1!) What do you have left when everything the first five books of the Bible have been preparing you for ends in a funeral?

It is against this background of the death of 'Moses the Incomparable' that the writer sets the continuity of Yahweh's promise. 'Moses my servant has died, so you must wait' ? No. 'You must weep' ? No. But, 'Rise, cross over ... into the land.' Moses may die; God's promise lives on. There is the passing

---

[1] Regarding the borders of the promised land noted in verse 4, see Yohanan Aharoni and Michael Avi-Yonah, *The MacMillan Bible Atlas*, rev. ed. (New York: Macmillan, 1977), 41; Yohanan Aharoni, *The Land of the Bible: A Historical Geography*, rev. and enl. (Philadelphia: Westminster, 1979, 67-77; and Gordon J. Wenham, *Numbers*, Tyndale Old Testament Commentaries (Leicester: Inter-Varsity, 1981), 231-33. Never in her history did Israel occupy the extent of territory described in Joshua 1:4.

of an era yet the endurance of the promise. Yahweh's fidelity does not hinge on the achievements of men, however gifted they may be, nor does it evaporate in the face of funerals or rivers.[2]

The Encouragement of Yahweh's Presence (1:5, 9, 17)

Secondly, Joshua 1 highlights the encouragement of Yahweh's presence. 'I will be with you' (v. 5). It is interesting to note that these simple words were spoken once before to a very reticent, backward, excuse-making, ask-George-not-me sort of fellow, that is, Moses, in Exodus 3:12, when he was called to face both Israel and pharaoh. The same God now gives the same assurance in similar threatening circumstances to Joshua. Indeed, a case can be made for the name *Yahweh* being intended as theological (or devotional) shorthand for the implications and message of the statement 'I will be with you' (see Exod. 3:14-15 in light of 3:12).[3] Hence Moses has died, but Yahweh has not changed. He is still Yahweh, the God who is *present* with his servant and his people to help and deliver (contrast Hosea 1:9).

It is because of this assurance that Yahweh can exhort Joshua to 'be strong and bold' (vv. 6, 7, 9). Joshua is not told to grit his teeth and screw up his courage on his own; he is to be strong only because Yahweh is with him (v. 9) and not because Yahweh prefers leaders who are positive thinkers. Note how this assurance keeps reappearing throughout the book (2:24; 3:7, 10; 4:14; 6:27; 10:14, 42; 13:6; 14:12; 21:44; 23:3, 10).

---

[2] John Calvin nicely stated the matter: 'This suggests the very useful reflection, that while men are cut off by death, and fail in the middle of their career, the faithfulness of God never fails. On the death of Moses a sad change seemed impending; the people were left like a body with its head lopped off. While thus in danger of dispersion, not only did the truth of God prove itself to be immortal, but it was shewn in the person of Joshua as in a bright mirror, that when God takes away those whom he has adorned with special gifts, he has others in readiness to supply their place, and that though he is pleased for a time to give excellent gifts to some, his mighty power is not tied down to them, but he is able, as often as seemeth to him good, to find fit successors, nay, to raise up from the very stones persons qualified to perform illustrious deeds' (*Commentaries on the Book of Joshua*, trans. Henry Beveridge, in vol. 4 of *Calvin's Commentaries*, 22 vols. [reprint ed.; Grand Rapids: Baker, 1981], xix).

[3] See Morris S. Seale, *The Desert Bible* (New York: St. Martin's, 1974), 154-56; Moshe Greenberg, *Understanding Exodus* (New York: Behrman House, 1969), 81-82; and Karl-Heinz Bernhardt, 'Hayah', *TDOT*, 3:380-81.

A contemporary Christian reader might see this and say that's all very nice for Joshua, but he was a noteworthy character; he had to lead all of Israel. What about the plain Christian like me? Is this promise for ordinary Christians? Look at the use of this promise in Hebrews 13:5-6:

> Keep your life free from love of money,
> and be content with what you have;
> for he has said, 'I will never fail you nor forsake you.'
> Hence we can confidently say,
> 'The Lord is my helper,
> I will not be afraid;
> what can man do to me?' [RSV].

Here the promise of Joshua 1:5 is applied to a Christian congregation. The promise of God's abiding presence in Joshua 1 is also for you (note the 'for' in Hebrews 13:5b) and is the solution to the sin of covetousness and discontent, which in turn (note the 'hence' of Hebrews 13:6) leads to the great freedom of life without fear! There is nothing more essential for the people of God than to hear their God repeating to them amid all their changing circumstances, 'I will be with you' or 'I will not forsake you.'

The Centrality of Yahweh's Word (1:7-8)
The third theme we observe is the centrality of Yahweh's word. Joshua is commanded to be especially strong and bold 'to be careful to do according to all the torah (instruction) which Moses my servant commanded you' (v. 7). God does not withhold the formula that leads to such obedience: 'you shall meditate (mutter) over this torah document day and night, so that you will be careful to do according to all that is written in it' (v. 8). Constant, careful absorbing of the word of God leads to obedience to it. Lack of study results in lack of obedience. Notice how the writer stresses this urgency of obedience to Yahweh's word in the last chapters as well (22:5; 23:6; cf. 8:30-35).

This command is given specifically to Joshua as the leader of God's people. Can we legitimately assume that it also obligates every Israelite or Christian? Yes. If we don't like

Joshua 1:7-8, we still have to face Psalm 1:2, which describes what should be true of every godly believer (i.e. 'but his delight is in Yahweh's torah, and in his torah he meditates day and night'). There is no escape! Indeed, the torah should be our delight. Life in the kingdom of God must be lived out of the Word of God. Joshua 1 and Psalm 1 alike tell us that a life pleasing to God does not arise from mystical experiences or warm feelings or from a new gimmick advocated in a current release from one of our evangelical publishers; no, it comes from the word God has already spoken and from obedience to that word.

The Unity of Yahweh's People (1:12-18)

Finally, Joshua 1 uses much space to describe the unity of Yahweh's people. One might think there is little theological meat in these verses, but when they are read in light of Numbers 32 they take on new significance. When the two (or two and one-half) tribes request Moses to assign them an inheritance to the east of the Jordan, Moses suspects that their query hides a fresh conspiracy to abort the fulfilment of God's promise. In a flash of white heat he lambastes them as a 'brood of sinful men' (Num. 32:14), apparently content to possess their land now, sit out the Cis-jordan conquest, allow the other tribes to fend for themselves, and thus to discourage and dishearten (Num. 32:7) the majority of God's people. So, Moses says, there will be another Kadesh-barnea! Numbers 13–14 all over again! It is in the light of the peril of rebellion against Yahweh that the unity of God's people becomes so crucial (Num. 32:16-27).

Now perhaps we can see why the unity of all Israel portrayed in Joshua 1 was so critical. Here Reuben. Gad, and half-Manasseh are models of willing obedience and instruments of encouragement. Indifference on their part or snubbing their noses at the western tribes would have discouraged and disheartened the rest of God's people and led to rebellion and unbelief. It is interesting to note the concern for 'all Israel' throughout the Book of Joshua (chs. 3–4; chs. 7–8; 10:29ff.; 22:12, 16; 23:2; 24:1).[4]

One can detect implications here for the doctrine and practice of the church – unity among God's people is no idle luxury. This does not mean that we have to feel all sticky and gooey about each other, but it does mean that we must care enough that we don't want any of the Lord's children to get discouraged. It seems that such caring encouragement should take place in our public meetings (Heb. 10:25; see a beautiful example in 1 Sam. 23:16). And it is crucial because, ultimately, unity is a prerequisite for fidelity.

So Moses has died. But Yahweh has not left Israel – or us – orphans; we still have God's promise, God's presence, God's Word, and God's people. And that should be enough until the kingdom of God comes in power and great glory.

The Promise of God and the Last Three Funerals (24:29-33)
These verses seem to be a rather dry-as-dust way to end an otherwise interesting book: an obituary column for a conclusion. However, we should ask why the writer closes his book this way. Does he want merely to supply burial details, provide a 'where they are now' section about the main cast, or furnish information so that relatives can find the right graves for Veterans' Day each year? I propose that these are theological obituaries and that the writer has deliberately placed them at the end of the book to underscore his concerns.

The Veracity of Yahweh's Promise
First, he emphasizes the veracity of Yahweh's promise. Observe the places where Joshua, the bones of Joseph, and Eleazar are said to be buried (vv. 30, 32, 33). Obviously a definite location is given in each case, but the important point is that each of them is buried *in the land* that Yahweh promised them. They have died; but their tombstones are monuments to the fidelity of Yahweh to his promise of the land.

The reference to the 'bones of Joseph' is particularly interesting (v. 32). The Book of Genesis closes with Joseph clinging to God's promise of the land. It is an astounding picture. Joseph is both over Egypt and in Egypt but certainly not of Egypt; for even as he dies his eyes are glued to another

---

[4] The unity of Israel throughout the Book of Joshua will form a healthy contrast to the increasing fragmentation of Israel in the Book of Judges.

land, which Yahweh has promised. He is so taken with that promise – it is such a passion with him – that he requires his kin to take his bones to that land when God leads them out of Egypt (cf. Heb. 11:22), which they did (Exod. 13:19). And now (Josh. 24:32) they find their resting place.

A tremendous amount of time has elapsed since Abraham received the promise – 500 to 600 years! But, so our writer avers, the passage of time does not void the promises of God. Joshua, Joseph, Eleazar – these, being dead, yet speak.

The Test for Yahweh's People

Secondly, our writer hints at the test for Yahweh's people. Verse 31 seems to be both positive and negative: 'Israel served Yahweh all the days of Joshua and all the days of the elders who outlived Joshua, who had known all the work of Yahweh that he had done for Israel.' Here is a record of fidelity and a hint of wavering. In this section we hear of the deaths of both Joshua and Eleazar. The Book of Joshua constantly links Eleazar and Joshua (14:1; 17:4; 19:51; 21:1) just as the Pentateuch links Aaron and Moses. Thus the deaths of Eleazar and Joshua signify the complete passing of that conquest generation. So the question lingers: Whither Israel? Will Israel still serve Yahweh now that Joshua and Eleazar and the elders are gone? In verse 31 the writer already seems to see the situation of Judges 2:10 and fears the answer is no.[5] (Maybe that's why he wrote this book – to depict the fidelity of Yahweh so that a wavering Israel might respond in kind before it was too late.)

Can the church remain faithful after the eyewitnesses are gone? That is no small test. Here is the continual danger of second-generation religion: Will we remain warm and faithful without the gentle pressure of our spiritual mentors on whom we once leaned? Although we ourselves have not seen the cutting off of the Jordan and the crumbling of Jericho, can we still cling to the God who did these acts?

---

[5] As Calvin states (*Joshua*, 282): 'Accordingly, attention is indirectly drawn to their inconstancy, when it is said that they served the Lord while Joshua survived, and till the more aged had died out. For there is a tacit antithesis, implying lapse and alienation, when they were suddenly seized with a forgetfulness of the Divine favours.'

The Need for Yahweh's Victory

Third, perhaps we are not wrong in seeing here the need for Yahweh's victory. True, these graves witness to the fulfilment of Yahweh's promise and yet there is an incompleteness, a tragedy about it, since it is marked by death. Why does Israel's saga of faith and life have to keep closing its chapters with death notices? Genesis ends with Joseph's death. Deuteronomy ends with Moses' death. The Book of Joshua ends with Joshua's death. Is this not the sting of sin we see here amid the fidelity of God? Is this not a sign of the wrath of God against us (Ps. 90:9, 11-12)? How much better when the One who 'abolished death' (2 Tim. 1:10) causes the last chapters to shimmer with resurrection (Matt. 28; Mark 16; Luke 24; John 20–21).

Study Questions:

1. Have you ever felt like your end was near but you needed to trust God's promises?

2. In what was has God reassured you of his presence, of his never "leaving you or forsaking" you?

3. How does the centrality of God's word make a difference in your life?

4. How were the tribes of Reuben, Gad and the half-tribe of Manasseh able to encourage all of Israel?

5. What particular promises of God have caused you to hang on in the midst of the impossible?

2

How to Listen to a Shady Lady Story
(Joshua 2)

For a proper understanding of the Rahab story we must pay careful attention to how it is put together.

Commission by Joshua, 1a
    Arrival/concern: protection of the spies, 2-7
        Confession of faith, 8-14
    Escape/concern: protection of Rahab and Co., 15-21
Return to Joshua, 22-24

The Confession of Yahweh's Sovereignty (2:8-14)
Now that we have this structure in front of us, let us ponder the major teaching of the chapter. This structure will help us to see that, first of all, the story underscores the confession of Yahweh's sovereignty. One might think of this structure as a sandwich, with the first and fifth sections representing the slices of bread, the second and fourth sections the pieces of lettuce, and the third or middle section the meat. Obviously, the meat is the most important – and expensive – part of the sandwich; the lettuce is extra and the bread is simply to keep the mayonnaise from getting all over one's hands. In this way the writer seems to tell us that he thinks verses 8-14 are the most important part of his story.

But, you might say, just because that section is in the middle of things doesn't necessarily mean that is what the writer thinks is most crucial. Can't we find some other clue? Yes, we can. Note how the writer creates suspense at the end of verse 7; he leaves the reader asking the question, 'How in the world will those fellows get out of the city when the gates have been shut?' If one really gets wrapped up in the story, that is precisely the anxiety one feels at the end of verse 7! But note that this tension is not relieved (that is, you don't get your literary Rolaid) until verse 15, where, at last, the question is answered. In between the writer places Rahab's confession of faith (vv. 8-13). This is an important mark of the writer's style. It is as if he is telling you, the reader: 'Don't bother your head about how those two fellows will escape; there is something *far more important* that I want to tell you; here, let me quote....' It is the writer's way of indicating that what Rahab is about to say is so important that all other matters must be placed on the back burner for now.

This, incidentally, tells us what the writer is *not* concerned about. He is not very interested in picky ethical questions based on verses 4-6: endless wranglings and discussions about whether it was right for Rahab to lie to the Jericho police, and so on. It is tragic when people snag their pants on the nail of Rahab's lie, quibble endlessly about the matter, and never get around to hearing Rahab's *truth* (vv. 8-13), which the writer has conspired to make the centre of the whole narrative. That is like a wife who proudly opens the refrigerator door to show her husband the scrumptious salad and dessert she has prepared for their dinner guests; but her husband, scarcely glancing at those delicacies, instead rubs his finger across the top of the fridge and goes off muttering that 'there seems to be a good bit of dust on the top of the refrigerator'. He missed the whole point! He didn't understand his wife's intention at all. His focus was all wrong. Naturally, the New Testament does not fall into this trap. It consistently stresses the *faith* of Rahab (Heb. 11:31; James 2:25).[1]

---

[1] This does not mean that the biblical writer necessarily approves of Rahab's lie or that he authorizes us to go and do likewise. He neither approves nor disapproves of Rahab's lie; rather, he ignores it (i.e. its ethical implications). Of course, Bible readers must always be careful to distinguish between what the Bible reports and what it recommends, between what it records and what it requires. The Bible reports that Jacob had four wives; it is hardly encouraging us to do the same.

The Might of Yahweh (2:10)

The content of Rahab's confession justifies its central place in the story. She rehearses the might of Yahweh: 'For we have heard how Yahweh dried up the waters of the Sea of Reeds before you when you came out of Egypt and what he did to the two Amorite kings on the other side of the Jordan – to Sihon and Og – whom you destroyed' (v. 10). This was the basis of her faith; she had heard about the mighty acts of God. This is the normal way of coming to faith. Biblical faith is based on at least some knowledge, data, and evidence. Even couples who 'fall' in love don't come to love each other merely by sighing or groaning or oohing and ahhing; rather they talk, communicate, find out about each other – their past, their likes, their dislikes, their character, and so on. Even romance has some basis in knowledge. So is the case with faith. Faith is not just a warm, cosy feeling about God. Faith grows, if at all, out of hearing what God has done for his people.

The Majesty of Yahweh (2:11)

Then Rahab confesses the majesty of Yahweh when she says that 'Yahweh your God is God in heaven above and upon earth below' (v. 11). That is the conviction of faith. This was to be the conclusion Israel was to reach about her God (Deut. 4:39). But here is a pagan, Canaanite harlot with an 'Israelite' confession on her lips. She holds to the utter supremacy of Yahweh. She seems to assume that he is the only God functioning in heaven and upon earth.

The Mercy of Yahweh (2:12-13)

All of this leads Rahab to seek the mercy of Yahweh: 'And now, swear an oath to me by Yahweh that, since I have acted faithfully toward you, you also shall act faithfully with my father's house and shall give me a reliable sign and shall save alive my father, mother, brothers, sisters, and all their families and shall deliver our lives from death' (vv. 12-13). Here is the evidence of faith. Genuine faith never rests content with being convinced of the reality of God but presses on to take refuge in God. Rahab not only must know the clear truth about God but also must escape the coming wrath of God. It isn't just a matter of correct belief but of desperate need. Saving faith is always like this. It never stops with brooding over the nature or activity of God but always runs to take refuge under his wings. Amazingly, Rahab not only trembles before the terror of the Lord but also senses that there might be mercy in this fearful God. What but the touch of Yahweh's hand could have created such faith in the heart of this pagan harlot?

Encouragement in Yahweh's Faithfulness

Secondly, this story shows that Israel is given encouragement in Yahweh's faithfulness. The net gain from the whole episode appears in the spies' report in verse 24: 'Surely Yahweh has given all the land into our hands; indeed, all the residents of the land melt in fear because of us.' The land has continued to be the concern of chapter 2 (vv. 1, 9, 14, 18, 24). And now as the fruit of the spies' reconnaissance the Israelites are assured that Yahweh will give them the land as promised. That is all. They formed no fifth column in the city – no one to do an 'inside job' and deliver the city by treachery. The only thing they received from the episode was to be sure of Yahweh's promise. Someone might say that they should have been certain of the promise without this extra encouragement. True, Yahweh's word is adequate in itself. The problem, however, is not that Yahweh's promises are not sure but that we need to *feel sure* of them. His word should be sufficient to bolster us. But because of the weakness of our faith, he graciously stoops down and by a plethora of signs, evidences, and providences makes us feel assured of his already sure word. It is something like a husband who sends a card or note through the mail to his wife telling her how much she means to him. She shouldn't need that to know that he loves her, but it is an extra effort that makes her feel loved and appreciated. So Yahweh understands our needs.

The Beauty of Yahweh's Grace

The beauty of Yahweh's grace is a final emphasis in the teaching of this chapter.

As a preliminary point, observe that chapter 2 is really non-essential for telling the story of Israel's entrance into the land. In fact, it would seem more logical to follow chapter 1 with chapter 3 immediately; this would make for a coherent narrative, with chapter 3 immediately fulfilling the expectations one has as he finishes reading chapter 1. (Someone will say, yes, but there is that little section in chapter 6 that mentions Rahab's rescue. True, but that section, verses 22-25, could easily have been excluded without any disturbance to the flow of the narrative.) The fact that the writer deliberately turns aside to insert and relate the Rahab story shows that it must carry special significance for him. Why would he go out of his way, as it were, to select this material?

This story then involves the conversion of a pagan – a Canaanite, even a harlot. The word for harlot here is *zonah* (v. 1). It is the usual Hebrew term for a harlot or prostitute. It could be that Rahab was actually a *qedeshah*, one of the sacred prostitutes who served at the Canaanite fertility shrines. But in biblical morality there was little difference between a holy whore and a plain whore. So Rahab is a *zonah* – a pagan and a disreputable one at that – yet she is welcomed into the church (6:22-25)! 'But Rahab the harlot ... Joshua saved alive; and she dwelt in Israel to this day' (6:25).

Now that can be offensive. We say we can't have that; the church is only for respectable, clean, middle-class folks. But that is like saying that hospitals are only for doctors, nurses, and x-ray machines instead of sick people. Or it is like saying that only morticians and coroners belong in morgues instead of dead people. Who then should be in the church but sinners? The church is not a club but a refuge for sinners who have been touched by the grace of God. Apparently, Rahab's past did not bother the writer of the first Gospel. Rather, Matthew seemed to see in Rahab a trophy of divine grace. Astounding, isn't it, that the shady lady of Jericho should be the ancestress of Jesus the Messiah (Matt. 1:5)?

Study Questions:

1. Do you think that Rahab acts in true faith in Yahweh or out of fear for her life?

2. Rahab moved from knowledge of Yahweh to trust in Yahweh. How did she express this?

3. How do you move from knowledge of Yahweh to trust in Yahweh? How did you express this?

4. God is faithful. What ways has God specifically shown himself to be faithful to you? What were the circumstances?

5. How does the story of Rahab encourage you in your relationship with Christ?

3

Going Across the Flow
(Joshua 3–4)

A cartoon in a Christian periodical depicts four priests carrying the ark of the covenant and approaching the Jordan River. One priest turns to his fellow and, with a look of fear, asks, 'Did you stop to think of how silly we're going to look if Joshua is wrong?' Naturally, the cartoon is noncanonical. But Joshua's prediction was a mouthful: 'And as soon as the priests who carry the ark of the LORD – the Lord of all the earth – set foot in the Jordan, its waters flowing downstream will be cut off and stand up in a heap' (3:13, NIV). Quite a feat for feet – even priests'!

Literary Features of the Narrative
Scholars have frequently been baffled by the apparent inconsistencies of Joshua 3–4. One does have problems putting together a neat structure for the story and understanding certain apparently isolated features (e.g. 3:12; 4:9). The real critical problems, however, are not nearly as aggravated as have been imagined.[1] Here it will suffice to point out those literary features that will aid us in appreciating and interpreting the story.

For one thing, there is a good deal of suspense built into this story. For example, when Yahweh instructs Joshua in 3:8, one

---

[1] See Paul P. Saydon, 'The Crossing of the Jordan, Josue 3; 4', *Catholic Biblical Quarterly* 12 (1950): 194-207.

expects to get more information as to what to expect next. But Yahweh's instructions end abruptly with the priests standing in the Jordan. Joshua's words (3:13) pick up and fill out that gap. Yet there is similar abruptness in 3:13, for although Joshua in his speech gives some additional information, he does not spell out exactly what is to occur after the waters stand in one heap. I will later call attention to the suspense in 3:15.

Secondly, note the attention given to the securing of the twelve memorial stones – and their significance (4:1-10a). The sections immediately before and after 4:1-10a describe the process of 'crossing over' ('*abar*; four times in 3:13-17, five times in 4:10b-14), but the major focus centres on the twelve stones:

Crossing over, 3:14-17
    Twelve stones, 4:1-10a
Crossing over, 4:10b-14

In 3:17 the priests are standing in mid-Jordan as the people cross over. In 4:10a they are still standing there. In one sense the story has not advanced. Moreover, 4:10b ('then the people hurried and crossed over') and 4:11a ('Now it came about when all the people finished crossing over...') return and pick up the strand of the narrative that was dropped at 3:17b and 4:1a just before the writer turned aside to recount the episode of the twelve stones. It appears that the writer deliberately intrudes the story about the stones into the narrative about the crossing because he intended us to realise it had special importance.

Thirdly, observe that the writer has placed Joshua's didactic speech at the very end of the episode (4:21-24). He reserves the heaviest accent until the end. Here is the theological concentrate of the Jordan crossing, the climactic homiletical conclusion that must stick in the heart of each Israelite. The same way of indicating stress can be seen in Matthew's report of the Lord's Prayer (Matt. 6:9-13). Matthew places Jesus' teaching on forgiveness immediately afterward (6:14-15) and so places special emphasis on the petition for pardon.

Keeping these items in mind, let us hear the witness our writer bears.

Theological Concerns of the Narrative

The Perception of Yahweh's Work (3:1-6)
In 3:1-6 the writer relates the various preparations Israel makes before entering the land. Here he emphasises the perception of Yahweh's work.

Before developing this point, however, we must observe the central role of the ark of the covenant in the whole episode. It appears first in verse 3 ('When you see the ark of the covenant of Yahweh your God, and the levitical priests carrying it, then *you* are to set out from your place and follow it'). It is mentioned seventeen times in these two chapters. Our writer refuses to allow us to lose sight of it! Thus the ark – sign of Yahweh's presence among his people – meets us at every turn, reminding us that it is Yahweh himself who leads his people into Canaan, who cuts off flooding waters and holds them back as it were with his hand.[2] The whole affair is Yahweh's feat and the Israelites, though active, are still primarily spectators.

Now, how is Israel to perceive Yahweh's work? From a distance, verse 4 seems to say: 'Only there is to be a distance between you and it [the ark], a distance of about 2,000 cubits; don't go near it, in order that you may know the way in which you are to go....' My translation follows the order of the Hebrew text, which most naturally suggests that the reason for the distance from the ark is in order that the people can tell where to go and can witness the cutting off of the Jordan, something they could not do if everyone was closely following the priests and the ark. But this way all could see Yahweh's great deed and all could know the path to take. This view is more satisfactory than seeing the awful holiness of the ark as the reason for the distance, as the Revised Standard Version and the New International Version do. They regard the distance clause as a parenthesis and place it at the end of the verse. There is a majestic holiness about Yahweh's presence signified in the ark (cf. 2 Sam. 6), but that does not seem to be the point here.[3]

---

[2] On the ark, see Exodus 25:10-22 and Numbers 10:33-36. For more detail, see J. Barton Payne, 'Ark of the Covenant', *ZPEB*, 1:305-10.

[3] On Joshua 3:3-4, see C. F. Keil, *Joshua, Judges, Ruth,* Biblical Commentary on the Old Testament (1868; reprint ed.; Grand Rapids: Eerdmans, 1950), 40-41; and F.

Not only distance but attitude was important for perceiving Yahweh's work. 'Sanctify yourselves, for tomorrow Yahweh will do wonders among you' (v. 5). What did this demand entail? From other occurrences (e.g. Exod. 19:10, 14, 22; Num. 11:18; Josh. 7:13; 1 Sam. 16:5), it means the special preparation demanded of the people whenever Yahweh was to reveal himself in a special way. It could include washing the clothes and abstaining from sexual relations; likely confession of sins as well. In short, when the Lord comes his people must be prepared.

But why all the bother about the distance and attitude? Why all the fuss over preparation for the big event? Because it is crucial that Israel recognise that what happens is indeed Yahweh's work; and unless they have proper insight, expectancy, and preparation, they could see Yahweh's work and yet not understand its true value and significance.

Several years ago my brother and I visited the Civil War battlefield at Antietam Creek near Sharpsburg, Maryland. There a park ranger took us to a second-floor room with windows all round and, using several giant mural maps, gave us a fascinating, informative lecture on the whole 1862 conflict. He brought the cornfield, the Dunker Church, Burnside, McClellan, and Lee wonderfully to life. At the close of his lecture – which came all too soon – I felt I had a grip on the pattern of the conflict that took place there. Without that preparation a drive around or hike over the battlefield would have been but historical bits and pieces not properly appreciated. As it was, I had been prepared because I had been given a perspective from which to view the event and its artifacts.

This is also true of Joshua 3–4. God's people must be rightly prepared for God's 'show' if they are going to appreciate it, if they are going to be fortified in faith. And, although Yahweh may not now cut a path through rivers for his people every month or so, the principle remains. Do you prepare yourself for the practice of the public worship of God? If we are not impressed with the grandeur of the living God in public worship, is it because we

---

R. Fay, *The Book of Joshua*, Lange's Commentary on the Holy Scriptures, in vol. 2, *Numbers–Ruth* (1870; reprint ed.; Grand Rapids: Zondervan, 1960), 56.

have not prepared ourselves to see him as such? Could it be that we even fail to detect the Lord's marvelous working in the routine affairs of our lives simply because we have not prepared ourselves to see or even expect that?

The Exaltation of Yahweh's Servant (3:7-9)

The exaltation of Yahweh's servant is a second major emphasis. Before the crossing Yahweh had assured Joshua, 'This day I will begin to exalt you in the eyes of all Israel, so that they will know that as I have been with Moses, so I will be with you' (3:7). Later the writer certifies that Yahweh was as good as his word: 'On that day Yahweh exalted Joshua in the eyes of all Israel, so that they feared him as they had feared Moses all the days of his life' (4:14). Given the crisis of Moses' death, the transition of leadership (see the exposition of ch. 1), and the struggle for conquest that lay ahead, it was crucial that Joshua feel secure in his position and that Israel be confident of his competence under God.

We may not initially see why this authentication of leadership is so important. Its importance is more apparent when confidence in leadership is lacking. Bruce Catton has described the attitude of the troops in General John Pope's army in the War Between the States. At one point they had been marched round and round, had outmarched their supplies so that most were hungry and exhausted, and were well aware that the high command was baffled and had the jitters. Hence the troops that Pope brought up to face Stonewall Jackson's guns were 'men who expected the worst and knew they were entitled to expect it'.[4] Why? Because they had absolutely no confidence in their leadership. God knew how vital his people's opinion of Joshua would be for the upcoming wars in Canaan; hence he stooped down that day both to dam up the river and to place his seal of competence upon his man Joshua.

The Assurance of Yahweh's Power (3:10-13)

The narrative also underscores the assurance of Yahweh's power. Before the crossing Joshua had predicted, 'By this

---

[4] Bruce Catton, *Mr. Lincoln's Army* (Garden City, N.Y.: Doubleday, 1951), 29, 34.

you will know that the living God is among you and he will certainly drive out from before you the Canaanites, Hittites, Hivites, Perizzites, Girgashites, Amorites, and Jebusites' (3:10). There is a certain logic behind this assurance. If Yahweh can tame a raging river, he can also repel attacking Amorites. If he can stop up the Jordan, he can put down the Girgashite. If he can get you into the land, he can surely give you the land. Paul uses the same 'theo-logic' in Romans 8:32 – if God did not hold back but gave up his own Son for us, if he went that far, can we not then rest assured that he will grant all other provisions required for our full salvation? It was the reasoning of faith that Israel failed to use in Exodus 16; they should have realised that the God who delivered them from Egypt (Exod. 14–15) would not let go of them in the wilderness. The rescue at the Red Sea, the crossing of the Jordan, and the death and resurrection of Christ are explosions of God's power that are meant to colour the whole horizon of the believer's life in order to assure us that the God who so mightily handles great emergencies is surely adequate for the smaller crises and anxieties that beset us.

'You will know that the living God is among you.' The object of this text then is to impress us with the adequacy of God, to grill into us that *God* is not merely a three-letter word of our Christian jargon, not merely the honorary leader of our club, but is the living God who works and intervenes and comes and saves and rescues and counsels his people in all their perplexities. He is indeed 'the Lord of all the earth' (vv. 11, 13), not a mere Little League deity. So we must renounce our tendency to 'punify' God, to carve him down to our stature and limit him to our possibilities.

The Strangeness of Yahweh's Method (3:14-17)

Fourthly, let us note the strangeness of Yahweh's method. Note especially verse 15c: 'The Jordan overflows all its banks throughout the time of harvest.' In the order of the Hebrew text (followed by rsv; but niv smooths out the text, wrongly, I think) verse 15c is a frustrating parenthesis in the report of the miracle.

Since Joshua has just assured us that the Jordan will stop flowing when the ark-bearing priests put their feet in the water

(v. 13), we begin reading 3:14ff. with real expectancy. Note how in verses 14ff. the writer builds clause by clause, detail by detail, to a certain point of tension – the point when the priests' feet dip into the water. Then, getting you on the edge of your chair, he does the most maddening thing. He supplies you with a little data on river conditions in springtime (v. 15c). (The effect is akin to watching a 1950s television drama in which hero and heroine are closing in for a climactic kiss, only to be cut off by a Rice Krispies commercial.) By doing so he – however briefly – delays the climax the reader longs for.[5] This latter is given in 16a: 'then the waters coming down from above stopped flowing'. The pattern is this:

Introduction, 14a
> 'When the people set out from their tents to cross...'

Clauses building to climax, 14b-15b
> First clause, 14b
>> 'and the priests, the bearers of the ark, were before the people'
> Second clause, 15a
>> 'and when the bearers of the ark came to the Jordan'
> Third clause, 15b
>> 'and the feet of the priests, the bearers of the ark, were dipped in the edge of the water'

Parenthesis delaying climax, 15c
> '(now the Jordan overflows its banks all the days of harvest)'

Resolution/continuation, 16a
> 'The waters coming down from above stopped flowing...'

Why would anyone want to ruin a perfectly good story with a report on river conditions? Because the river helps one to appreciate the miracle.

The actual Jordan Valley between the Sea of Galilee and the Dead Sea varies in breadth from 3 to 14 miles. Within this valley is the river's floodplain, which is 200 yards to 1 mile wide. The

---

[5] See Marten H. Woudstra, *The Book of Joshua*, The New International Commentary on the Old Testament (Grand Rapids: Eerdmans, 1981), 86-87.

floodplain was packed with tangled bush and jungle growth. Hence 'it was not the river so much as the jungle that was difficult to cross, the fords of the Jordan being as much ways through the jungle as through the river'.[6] Then there was the river channel itself, which – if similar to nineteenth-century (AD) conditions – was from 90 to 100 feet broad, with a depth of 3 feet at some fords to as much as 10 to 12 feet. The current was strong because of the drop in elevation (a drop of 40 feet per mile near the Sea of Galilee and an average of 9 feet per mile overall).[7]

This means that the river Israel faced that springtime was no placid stream but a raging torrent, probably a mile wide and covering a mass of tangled brush and jungle growth. So says verse 15c.

Such detail is important. When was it that God led Israel through the Jordan? Precisely at the time of year when such a feat looked and was impossible. Why does the God of the Bible insist on fording the river at the most unpropitious time? I am not sure. But this is a marked tendency in his ways. Yahweh delights to show his might in the face of our utter helplessness, apparently so that we cannot help seeing that we contribute nothing to our deliverance (cf. Judg. 7:2).

There is a strangeness about Yahweh's method, and yet there is a method in his 'madness'. Perhaps he brings us into impossible circumstances, situations so bleak and hopeless, for the very purpose of impressing upon us that if we make it through, if we endure it, if we are not overwhelmed and washed away, it will be only because of his grace and power. Is this his way of teaching us our own inability and helplessness in order that we may realise that our 'help comes from the Lord, who made heaven and earth' (Ps. 121:2)?

---

[6] H. L. Ellison, *Scripture Union Bible Study Books: Joshua–2 Samuel* (Grand Rapids: Eerdmans, 1966), 5.

[7] See George Adam Smith, *The Historical Geography of the Holy Land,* 22d ed. (London: Hodder and Stoughton, n.d.), 482-87, and W. M. Thomson, *The Land and the Book,* 2 vols. (New York: Harper and Brothers, 1873), 2:446, 449, 452-56. Two spies might cross the Jordan (Josh. 2), but a whole people with women, children, livestock, and possessions could not. Cf. 1 Chron. 12:15 (on river conditions).

The Remembrance of Yahweh's Goodness (4:1-10, 21-24)

Turning to chapter 4, we notice its stress on the remembrance of Yahweh's goodness. This chapter focuses on the twelve stones and their function. Getting through the river isn't the end of it all; you must remember what happened there. We can catch the main intention from verses 6-7:

> In order that this may be a sign among you, when your sons ask you in the future, 'What do these stones mean to you?,' then you shall say to them: 'The waters of the Jordan were cut off from before the ark of the covenant of Yahweh; when it crossed into the Jordan, the waters of the Jordan were cut off.'

We observe a certain assumption operating in 4:1-10, namely, that the greatest enemy of faith may be forgetfulness (cf. Deut. 8). Just as in a marriage, the real threat may not be infidelity but simply a slow process of forgetting and a gradual failure to remember the preciousness of the other person. So, Joshua says, you must remember what Yahweh has done; and these stones are to serve as visual aids to that end.

Furthermore, Israel must not only remember for themselves but teach their children to remember (4:7, 21-24) as well. The twelve stones were meant to provide occasions for teaching, for impressing upon the next generation Yahweh's mighty act at the Jordan. We can almost see it now. Fifteen years post-Jordan time an Israelite father and his six-year-old son are strolling through Gilgal National Park. The lad spots an imposing pile of stones. He counts twelve, and exclaims, 'Hey, Daddy, what are those stones for?' The son's curiosity now becomes the occasion for communicating to him the news of Israel's astounding God and how he unleashed his power for his people.

There is an implication here. If Yahweh so insists that Israel remember this day, it implies that this event was unique and that Yahweh does not usually work with such visibly raw power. If Yahweh did something of this magnitude every fifth Wednesday or so, why should Israel need to remember Jordan Day? Apparently, this sort of miracle will be infrequent. Yahweh's standard method of retaining his people's fidelity is not by frequent and dazzling displays of power but by faithful witness and teaching of those particular acts in which he had already demonstrated his care for his own.

The pattern of remembering carries over for the church. We continue to remember the utterly unique act of our Redeemer in the Lord's Supper. Even our children whisper to us as we take the elements, 'What does that mean? What is that? What are you doing?' And even there we can whisper our brief witness back to them. Why this remembrance? Lest we begin to regard the cross as a piece of furniture rather than the throne of the Shepherd who soaked up the wrath of God for the sins of his flock.

The Evidence of Yahweh's Hand (4:18)

More briefly, we should note how 4:18 reveals the evidence of Yahweh's hand. When 'the soles of the priests' feet were drawn out to dry ground, the waters of the Jordan returned to their place and went over all their banks as before'. Because of the timing there can be no doubt that the stoppage of the river was Yahweh's work. Clearly, it was no mere coincidence. How Yahweh stopped the Jordan, we do not know. Evidently, the Israelites knew where the stoppage occurred (3:16). The Jordan has been dammed since by collapse of banks or local earthquake. This happened in 1267, 1906, and 1927, the first for some ten hours, the last for over twenty-one hours.[8] Whether Yahweh used secondary causes, such as the caving in of high banks upstream, we cannot tell. That may have been the means he used. But who knows? And what does it matter? The precise timing of the return of the waters in 4:18 clearly intends us to understand the incident as a wonder done by God's hand.

The Date of Yahweh's Fidelity (4:19)

Finally, 4:19 inserts a little note on the date of Yahweh's fidelity. On the 'tenth day of the first month' the people went up from the Jordan and camped at Gilgal. C. F. Keil pointed out that it was on the same day forty years before that Israel had begun to prepare for going out of Egypt by setting apart the Passover

---

[8] John Gray, *Joshua, Judges and Ruth*, New Century Bible (Greenwood, S.C.: Attic, 1967), 63.

lamb (Exod. 12:2-3).[9] Therefore, we might say this day had marked the beginning of redemption; now it marked its completion. What Yahweh began he brought to completion. Yahweh has written his faithfulness across another date on our calendars! Israel had been a slave; now Israel was an heir.

There can be no doubt about the thrust of these chapters nor about the teaching Israel was to derive from this event. Joshua's preaching in 4:21-24 drives home the major point. Yahweh has done it again! He has put the Jordan River on the map of faith along with the Red Sea – so that gentile observers might have clear proof of his might and Israel might reverently and continually submit to his sway.

STUDY QUESTIONS:

1. What is the significance of the 12 stones plucked from the Jordan River?

2. Why do you think God made the crossing of the Jordan so 'grand'?

3. Do you prepare yourself to meet God in worship?

4. How has god recently displayed his power in your life?

5. Where do you notice the 'wonder' of god the most? When do you see his hand at work?

---

[9] Keil, *Joshua*, 51.

Part 2

Taking the Land

(Joshua 5–12)

4

Celebrating the Sacraments
(Joshua 5:1-12)

With chapter 5 we enter a new division of the Book of Joshua. Chapter 1 provided the prologue; entering the land was the theme of chapters 2–4. Chapters 5–12 deal with taking the land. We need not delay over structural matters now, though we may note in passing that the similar headings of 5:1, 9:1-2, 10:1-2, and 11:1-3 (each begins with kings or some king 'hearing' about Israel's or God's exploits) mark the major divisions of this material. Chapters 5–8 constitute a whole section, but it will prove more digestible to swallow it in somewhat smaller bites.

Before setting forth the teaching of 5:1-12, we should take a preliminary look at verses 2-9, the circumcision of the current generation. Verses 4-7 form the heart of this section and provide the rationale for the circumcision. These verses explain, in part, why the present generation of Israel had to be circumcised (vv. 4-5); they do not directly explain why they had *not* been circumcised before this time. The closest clue comes in verse 6 – the wilderness period was the time of unbelief and judgment (see Num. 14), a time for the old Israel to die and perish. The original exodus generation doomed themselves to wander forty years and perish in the wilderness (Num. 14:34-35). Some, therefore, infer that the sign of circumcision was likely withdrawn (by God) during the wilderness period as a sign of Yahweh's displeasure and that Israel was (as it were) on probation.[1] But this inference, though credible, goes a bit beyond the text and we cannot be sure that circumcision was withheld by divine direction. However, in light of Genesis 17:14, one can say that this lack of circumcision was a sign that Israel was 'cut off' (because of their unbelief?). They were God's people and yet they were not; they remained objects of God's care and yet possessed no sign to show they were his. These are brief words for a complex issue, but they must suffice.

Criticism of God's People (5:1-6a)

Our writer then asserts his criticism of God's people. What a note of irony there is in his description of the exodus generation: 'they had been circumcised' (v. 5a) yet they 'did not listen to the voice of Yahweh' (v. 6; see Num. 14:22). So they were 'finished off' (v. 6a). By contrast, their children 'were uncircumcised' and yet Yahweh 'raised (them) up' (v. 7). Hear the warning: 'They had been circumcised' but 'they did not listen to the voice of Yahweh'. You can have all the marks of the people of God but lack the response of the people of God. You can receive the sacrament but have no faith. Paul is right – you can experience the exodus, eat the manna, drink the water from the rock, and remain in unbelief (1 Cor. 10:1-5). You may hold membership among God's flock but have no relationship with the Shepherd. You may live in the King's country but reject his sovereignty.

Certainty of God's Promise (5:6b)

The text also affirms the certainty of God's promise. Note that in verse 6b there are two occurrences of 'Yahweh swore', which seem to be opposed to each other. The exodus generation did not listen to Yahweh's voice 'so that *Yahweh swore* to them that they would not see the land that *Yahweh swore* to their fathers to give us'. God's oath to Abraham, Isaac, and Jacob had been to

---

[1] See J. A. Motyer, 'Circumcision', *IBD*, 1:288-89, and Karl Gutbrod, *Das Buch vom Lande Gottes*, Die Botschaft des Alten Testaments, 3d ed. (Stuttgart: Calwer, 1965), 42. For the theology of circumcision, see especially Motyer's transcribed lectures. 'Old Testament Covenant Theology', 6-8 (Theological Students' Fellowship; not a formal publication).

give their descendants this land (see Exod. 32:13). Now God's oath prohibits a generation of their descendants from obtaining that land. Does this new oath negate the old oath? Not at all. Yahweh's promise of the land still holds, but one generation by its unbelief has forfeited its share in that promise. The promise will be fulfilled but unbelievers will not enjoy that fulfilment. One may say that unbelief might delay the fulfilment of God's promise, though I do not like to put it that way. What is crucial, however, is realising that Yahweh does fulfil his promises in spite of human unbelief. Unbelief may forfeit the benefits of the covenant promise but it cannot negate the promise.

I remember my father telling of doing the churning with his younger brother when they were boys. The normal procedure was to switch off, to take turns, as they did the churning. My father, however, discovered that if with some well-timed provocation he made his brother angry while the latter was churning, his brother would refuse to allow my father to take his turn and so do all the churning himself. So guess who would try to start a fight at churning time? But did the fighting cancel the churning? By no means! Whether by peace or by strife the churning was done. Without anger or through it the result was achieved.

Now that is – very roughly perhaps – the point here. Sometimes we view our God as a false god; we think that he is surely frustrated and furrow-browed over the roadblocks unbelief and disobedience pose to his bringing his kingdom. But the point of the text is that human rebellion cannot pack that sort of punch. Do you think man's unbelief can annul God's promise? The humiliating news is the essential powerlessness of human sin and rebellion. 'Yahweh swore ... Yahweh swore' (v. 6): that is the dynamic of the promise-keeping God.[2]

Continuity of God's Provision (5:10-12)
Lastly, we observe an emphasis on the continuity of God's provision. Now, as in Egypt, Israel celebrates the Passover;

---

[2] Cf. Walter C. Kaiser, Jr., *Toward an Old Testament Theology* (Grand Rapids: Zondervan, 1978), 156-57, for a similar approach to the Davidic covenant promise; God's promise to David persists even though some of David's successors are unfaithful.

there they had celebrated the beginning of redemption, now, in a sense, its completion. A new age really has begun.[3] No longer can the Egyptians crack their Hebrew jokes (v. 9).[4] However, the dominant emphasis lies in the fact that now Israel was eating of the produce of the land of Canaan, a fact that the writer mentions three times in verses 11-12. Now they enjoy what God was giving them in the land.

So the manna ceased (v. 12; see Exod. 16). They didn't need the manna now, as they did in the wilderness (cf. Exod. 16:35). Did that mean that Yahweh had quit providing for them? No, because 'they ate of the produce of the land of Canaan that year' (v. 12b). In the wilderness Israel had an extraordinary need and extraordinary needs frequently call forth God's unusual supply (e.g. manna). But now Israel is in the land – and there food grows in the ground, so it needn't come from heaven. The manna was God's special supply for an exceptional need. But now that the need becomes normal his provision comes by ordinary means. But it is still *his* provision, whether it is manna that falls from heaven in the wilderness or grain that grows in the ground in Canaan.

Clarence Macartney told the story about Dr. John Witherspoon's wisdom in this regard. Witherspoon was a signer of the Declaration of Independence and president of the (then) College of New Jersey. He lived a couple of miles away from the college at Rock Hill and drove a horse and rig each day to his office at the college. One day one of his neighbours burst into his office, exclaiming, 'Dr. Witherspoon, you must join me in giving thanks to God for his extraordinary providence in saving my life, for as I was driving from Rocky Hill the horse ran away and the buggy was smashed to pieces on the rocks, but I escaped unharmed!' Witherspoon replied,

---

[3] See Marten H. Woudstra (*The Book of Joshua*, The New International Commentary on the Old Testament [Grand Rapids: Eerdmans, 1981], 102-3) on the new beginning the writer intends to mark here.

[4] I follow C. F. Keil (*Joshua, Judges, Ruth*, Biblical Commentary on the Old Testament [1868; reprint ed.; Grand Rapids: Eerdmans, 1950], 59) in taking the 'reproach of Egypt' (v. 9) as the reproach, taunts, and ridicule that the Egyptians (at least could have) heaped upon the Israelites. Though Calvin regards this view as farfetched, usage of 'reproach' (*herpah*) in 'genitive' constructions supports it. Cf. Numbers 14:13-14.

'Why, I can tell you a far more remarkable providence than that. I have driven over that road hundreds of times. My horse never ran away, my buggy never was smashed, I was never hurt.'

So we must beware of thinking that God is only in the earthquake, wind, and fire; of thinking that manna but not grain is God's food. Most of God's gifts to his people are not dazzling and gaudy but wrapped in simple brown paper. Quiet provisions of safety on the highway, health of children, picking up a paycheck, supper with the family – all in an ordinary day's work for our God.

STUDY QUESTIONS:

1. How is it possible to 'hold membership among God's flock but have no relationship with the Shepherd?'

2. Does unbelief frustrate the promises of God or merely postpone them?

3. What is the difference between Israel eating in the wilderness and eating the Promised Land?

4. How have you seen God work in the ordinary ways in your life?

5. How have you seen God work in the extraordinary ways in your life?

5

Joshua Did *Not* Fight the
Battle of Jericho
(Joshua 5:13–6:27)

A well-known Christian periodical once published a cartoon that depicted a high-walled city in the background (probably Jericho) and two ancient military officers conferring over a plan of battle in the foreground. One officer turns to the other with the question: 'What would Jesus do?'

That punchline probably crystallizes how many folks feel about the biblical conquest. Doesn't God's command to Israel to invade Canaan and wipe out all its resisters run contrary to the mind and spirit of Jesus (whatever the latter is – most folks seem to leave it conveniently undefined, though it usually seems to mean 'not harsh and abrasive like the God of the Old Testament')? I have no passion to advance an apologetic for the conquest, but I do think it is important for us to understand the Old Testament's own perspective on the conquest.

In Genesis 15:16 Yahweh explained to Abram that his descendants would not inherit Canaan immediately but would come back in the fourth generation, 'for the iniquity of the Amorites is not yet complete'. The implication is that Yahweh was being patient with the present inhabitants of the land but that when their sins had reached the limit, he would use Abram's descendants to bring judgment upon them.

This view is confirmed in the rest of the Pentateuch. Yahweh cast out the residents of Canaan because of their gross sexual perversions (Lev. 18:24-25) and their zeal for magic, divination, and all such pagan hanky-panky (Deut. 18:12). Hence Israel must not assume a holier-than-you-all attitude, for Yahweh will not bring his people into the land because they are righteous and deserving; 'it is because of the wickedness of these nations that Yahweh is driving them out before you' (Deut. 9:4-5). The conquest is not a bunch of land-hungry marauders wiping out, at the behest of their vicious God, hundreds of innocent, God-fearing folks. In the biblical view, the God of the Bible uses none-too-righteous Israel as the instrument of his just judgment on a people who had persistently reveled in their iniquity. This will not answer all your dilemmas with the conquest, but you must see the Old Testament's view – the conquest is not gross injustice but the highest (and most patient [Gen. 15:16]) justice.[1] We will return to the question of the conquest later.

We now turn to the teaching of this section, including literary considerations where appropriate.

The Appearance of Yahweh's Help (5:13–6:5)
In 5:13–6:5 the writer depicts the appearance of Yahweh's help. These verses should be construed as a unit, the chapter division ignored, and 6:1 recognised as a parenthetical remark and placed within brackets.[2] Hence 6:2 picks up the flow from 5:15. On this view 6:2-5 contain the instructions of the captain of Yahweh's host; indeed the captain is identified with Yahweh (6:2a).

There is something both appropriate and strange about the appearance of Joshua's visitor (5:13-15): he is appropriate because he appears as a warrior. This is clear from the sword he wields (5:13) and the identity he discloses ('the Captain of Yahweh's army', 5:14). What a great comfort this must have

---

[1] See further Gustav Friedrich Oehler, *Theology of the Old Testament*, 8th ed. (New York and London: Funk and Wagnalls, 1883), 81-82.

[2] So C. F. Keil, *Joshua, Judges, Ruth,* Biblical Commentary on the Old Testament (1868; reprint ed.; Grand Rapids: Eerdmans, 1950), 63-64. Similar examples of parenthetical notes may be found in 3:15b and Judges 20:27b-28a.

been to a man and people about to carry on military conflict! Ultimate responsibility does not rest on Joshua's shoulders, nor are the twelve tribes the only army fighting for their cause.[3] The God of the Bible has a knack for tailoring the disclosures of his character to the various and particular needs of his people.

But there is also a strangeness about this captain. He does not fit any of Joshua's categories. But when Joshua receives the command to remove his sandals (5:15), he doubtless begins to sense who this unconventional soldier personage was.

We would do well to ask the import of this encounter. At least its primary function was not to give specific instructions but to bring about reverent submission. Sometimes we need to see that Yahweh is not so much partisan as sovereign, that it is more important to recognise God's position than to know God's plans. 'We can easily become more interested in special guidance than in a right relationship with the Guide.'[4]

Just because 6:1 is a parenthetical comment does not mean it is unimportant. It tells us that 'Jericho had shut the gate and was so completely closed to the Israelites that no one could go out or in' (Woudstra's translation). 'The purpose of this verse is to describe the seemingly hopeless situation confronting Israel, a people unskilled in the kind of warfare that was now required.'[5] This makes Yahweh's statement, 'See! I have given Jericho into your hand' (6:2), all the more surprising and encouraging. God's methodology is frequently like this. Greater obstacles for his people call forth his mighty help, even though we must admit that sometimes nothing looks quite so unlikely as the decree of God (6:2 in light of 6:1).

The Strangeness of Yahweh's Method (6:6-15)

We cannot help noticing the strangeness of Yahweh's method: armed men, seven priests blowing rams' horns, the ark, the rear guard, such was the caravan that circled Jericho

---

[3] Yahweh's army (or host, Hebrew, ṣaba', vv. 14, 15) probably refers to his angelic legions as in 1 Kings 22:19; Psalms 103:21; 148:2.

[4] H. L. Ellison, *Scripture Union Bible Study Books: Joshua – 2 Samuel* (Grand Rapids: Eerdmans, 1966), 6-7.

[5] Marten H. Woudstra, *The Book of Joshua*, The New International Commentary on the Old Testament (Grand Rapids: Eerdmans, 1981), 108.

each day and seven times on the seventh day. But, as at the crossing of the Jordan, it is the ark of Yahweh that holds centre stage. The chapter refers to the ark ten times, nine of which are in these verses. It is Yahweh's presence in the midst of his people that will make the difference. The people are not allowed to shout (6:10) until the given signal. So this little section stresses how central Yahweh's presence is and how passive God's people are. In this case God's people will not contribute to the overthrow (although they are involved in the following combat and mop-up [6:20-21]). Sometimes, it seems, God insists on bypassing his people's activity in order to enhance his own glory among his people. If Israel only marches and shouts, there will be no doubt about who batters Jericho to the ground. God still functions this way. His normal pattern is to work through the instrumentality of his people. But since we have this tendency to obscure God's splendor and to steal his praise, he sometimes sets our contributions aside, so that we – and others – can perceive that the 'overwhelming power comes from God and not from us' (2 Cor. 4:7, JB).

The Demand on Yahweh's People (6:16-21)

While we are considering strange items, we should also observe the demand on Yahweh's people.

Let us look at the way this little section is constructed. We already know both from Yahweh's instructions (6:5) and Joshua's command (6:10) that on the circuit of the seventh day – and only when given an explicit command – the people are to shout. After having read verses 10 and 16b ('And Joshua said to the people, "Shout!"'), one expects to hear the people shout as in verse 20. Indeed, in light of verse 10, the most natural sequence would be for verse 20 immediately to follow verse 16. (Joshua said, Shout [16]; then the people shouted [20].) In fact, after verse 16b the reader can hardly wait to hear the results. But the writer makes you wait. He uses a delayed climax by including Joshua's instructions and warnings (vv. 17-19) between Joshua's order to shout and the response to that command.[6]

---

[6] Ibid., 112.

If, as verse 10 asserts, the people were to shout when Joshua commanded 'Shout!' it is a bit awkward to assume that after 'Shout' in verse 16b the people quietly restrained themselves and attentively listened to: Joshua's continuing elaboration of the law of the ban;[7] the procedure for treating Rahab and company; and the warning against personal appropriation of Jericho's booty. Had they been poised for Joshua's 'Shout!' they surely would have obediently smothered his homily with their outburst!

What then am I suggesting, that verses 16c-19 are unhistorical, that Joshua never said them? No, I would hold that Joshua did give these instructions to Israel, but more likely, on a previous occasion. However, the writer in reporting Joshua's words inserted them after 'Shout' (v. 16b) and so constructed a delayed climax for a particular purpose. He does this because what Joshua says in verses 17-19 is more important than Jericho's walls falling down (v. 20). By such literary style the writer highlights the priority of obedience to Yahweh's commands over victory in itself. Just how crucial this is will appear in chapter 7 (Achan). Even in the victories God gives, there lurk temptations for his people.

This concern pertains to us as well. Like the disciple, we can be more taken up in preserving a fine mountain-top experience than in submitting to the sway of God's Chosen. And so our Father must admonish us: 'This is my Son ... listen to *him*' (Luke 9:35 and context).

No doubt, if someone were making a movie of Joshua 6 he would shoot extensive scenes of the actual assault of the city, combat scenes within, and so on. But our writer has no such celluloid interests nor does he care to show the bravado of Israelite warriors. He gives only a very brief mention, an almost matter-of-fact report, of the triumph itself (vv. 20b-21) – one and a half verses! This should clue us that his concerns lie elsewhere.

---

[7] To be 'under the ban' (NASB) or 'devoted for destruction' (RSV), Hebrew, *herem*, meant that people, places, and material were off limits for Israel and were to be 'devoted' (cf. NIV) only to Yahweh by destruction or – in the case of some goods – by placing them in Yahweh's treasury. See D. J. Wiseman, 'Ban', *IBD*, 1:171; R. P. Gordon, 'War', *IBD*, 3:1629; and Leon J. Wood, *TWOT*, 1:324-25. The operation of the ban shows that this conquest was primarily a religious assault, a true holy war and not a mere plundering bonanza to enrich Israel.

The Salvation in Yahweh's Judgment (6:22-25)

Lastly, our writer wants us to see the salvation in Yahweh's judgment (6:22-25). In between the notices of Jericho's destruction (vv. 21, 24) is a story of salvation and rescue (vv. 22-23, 25).[8] Rahab and her loved ones are salvaged and begin a life in association with God's people.[9] Rahab so feared Yahweh's threat that she fled to his mercy. Now she has received mercy. This pagan gentile and her family now stand within the circle of the chosen people. Why, then, should we be surprised if her God should one day take those who are far off and 'bring (them) near by the blood of the Messiah' (Eph. 2:13)?

STUDY QUESTIONS:

1. When is it the most difficult to view God in His sovereignty?

2. How have you seen God display his glory in uncommon ways?

3. Why does God often use the 'weak' things to bring about his purposes?

4. How has victory in your life also lead to temptation?

5. Are you ever 'surprised' when God chooses to save the 'poor and lowly' of this world? Wouldn't the rich and famous have more influence?

---

[8] On the problem of the archaeology of Jericho, see John J. Bimson, *Redating the Exodus and Conquest*, Journal for the Study of the Old Testament/Supplement Series 5 (Sheffield, 1978), 115-45. Bimson argues for his own proposal but also gives a good review of the problem and of previous work on Jericho. For the manner, problems, and historicity of the conquest, see the remarks later in this volume.

[9] Ellison, *Joshua – 2 Samuel*, 7, observes that 'the case of Rahab ... shows that any Canaanite could have saved his life by sincerely accepting God's will and repudiating his past'.

6

The Church in the Hands
of an Angry God
(Joshua 7)

About a year ago I was on a plane en route home. It happened to be a supper flight, but I became mildly perplexed when my meal was served. There were potatoes as part of the main dish and yet on the left side of the tray was a baked potato, unwrapped, with brown skin on display. While I ate the main course I pondered why the airline had served their potatoes-a-la-vengeance menu, since I have always considered airlines as having a good deal of class. However, when it came time to eat my baked potato, I discovered by both sight and touch that it was a wheat roll! That explained why the caterers had been so unsanitary in not wrapping a potato. I was sure I had a potato, but I was wrong. The apparent is not always the true.

Diving into Joshua 7 is a sort of potato-and-roll experience. We hardly get five verses into the chapter before we start thinking of how it alerts us to the peril of overconfidence and – some will infer – how it teaches us the danger of failing to pray. Here, we think, are some negative examples meant to teach us. Such is the apparent and, I think, wrong view.

It is important that we look carefully at the literary structure of Joshua 7. The writer displays a number of literary skills in this section,[1] but we confine ourselves to the overall literary structure:

Yahweh's wrath (burning), 1
   Disaster for Israel – defeat, 2-5
      Leaders before Yahweh – perplexity, 6-9
         Divine revelation of problem, 10-12a
            Mid-point, 12b
         Divine instruction for solution, 13-15
      Israel before Yahweh – clarity/exposure, 16-23
   Disaster for Achan – execution, 24-26a
Yahweh's wrath (turned away), 26b

Having set forth this structure and believing that it represents accurately the content of Joshua 7, I must nevertheless confess that I am a bit suspicious of it. It seems too neat. I am not sure that Old Testament writers deliberately constructed their narratives so that we could discover neat patterns in them, though literary artistry does pervade the Old Testament narratives. I would not, then, shed blood for all the details of this structure (though I do not think it is forced upon but comes from the text). But I will insist that observing the thematic inclusion about the wrath of Yahweh is crucial for a proper interpretation of chapter 7.

The Evidence of Yahweh's Wrath (7:1-5)
Now let us proceed to the teaching of the chapter while keeping this structure in mind. We observe that verses 1-5 emphasise the evidence of Yahweh's wrath. A number of expositors seem not to stress this point; instead it is common to look at these verses as reasons for Israel's failure at Ai. One popular exposition handles it this way:

---

[1] For example: (1) In 7:1 he informs the reader of the act of unfaithfulness, the identity of the culprit, and the wrath of Yahweh; yet an element of suspense remains because even with this tip-off the problem of divine wrath is not solved for the reader. (2) Note how the writer refrains from divulging certain items until a climactic time. Although he has indicated that some of the devoted stuff had been pilfered, he doesn't tell the reader exactly what that was. He allows Achan himself to particularise that in 7:21; this way the reader gets fresh information almost at the end of the story, which helps to sustain interest.

The first reason for failure at Ai ... was, manifestly, self-confidence. It was only a small city compared to Jericho ... and it seemed quite unnecessary for the whole army to attack it. A few thousand men would be sufficient, said those who had reconnoitered!

The second reason for the failure of Israel at Ai was, manifestly, neglect of prayer. It is quite clear, from the reading of the second verse, that Joshua at this moment failed to wait on God. He did not go back to Gilgal. Flushed with the victory at Jericho, he immediately made plans to capture the next portion of the territory. Had he prostrated himself in humility at the time when the people shouted for victory at Jericho, he would never have been humbled to the dust over the defeat at Ai.

These points will obviously preach, but they do not stay tied to the moorings of verses 1 and 26. In fact, one wonders how firm such expository inferences are when another expositor can look at verse 2 and, using the same method, come up with the opposite point:

Joshua did not rest on his oars, but proceeded to the task which lay before him, sending out scouts to examine the next place to be captured. After such a notable victory, he did not deem himself entitled to sit down and take things easy, or give himself to feasting; but believed in the policy of striking while the iron is hot.

So one expositor blames Joshua for acting without prayer while another commends him for acting with haste; one says it was bad that action was taken without prayer, yet the other claims it was good to have action without sloth. We are at hermeneutical sea unless we take seriously the writer's own intention as expressed in verse 1.

The framing of the narrative in terms of Yahweh's wrath (vv. 1, 26) supplies the theme and major category for the chapter; which means that verses 2-5 must be interpreted in light of verse 1. Therefore, verses 2-5 cannot be regarded as furnishing the reasons for Israel's failure at Ai. They failed because of Yahweh's anger. Their overconfidence – if it was such – was the result of Yahweh's anger leading them to destruction, not the reason for defeat. John Calvin discerned this:

When the three thousand or thereabouts were repulsed, it was only a just recompense for their confidence and sloth. The Holy Spirit, however, declares that fewness of numbers was not the cause of the discomfiture, and ought not to bear the blame of it. The true cause was the secret counsel of God, who meant to show a sign of his anger, but allowed the number to be small in order that the loss might be less serious.[2]

While the peril of overconfidence and the neglect of prayer are very preachable, they cannot be preached with authority from this text. The text says that God's people failed because they were under God's wrath. We must not trivialise this point with an improper response, as though we have played with and solved the intellectual puzzle of what Joshua 7 is about. Yahweh's wrath is not a mere theme; rather the church must tremble before it. What makes us think that Israel is the only congregation who has been or is under the wrath of God? 'True Israelites tremble when God is angry.'[3]

The Perplexity Under Yahweh's Wrath (7:6-9)
Secondly, note the perplexity under Yahweh's wrath. There's no difficulty understanding Israel's quandary. Their defeat at Ai (vv. 4-5) was a shock, wholly unexpected. They had been 'standing on the promises' (3:10) – and now this. No wonder their 'hearts melted' (v. 5; contrast 2:11; 5:1) as they anticipated their own destruction (v. 9).

Sometimes Joshua is riddled with expository bullets because of the tone and complaint of his prayer. But these are cheap shots. We must remember that Joshua has not yet received the information of verse 1. We have; the writer has informed us at the beginning. I call this having the reader's edge. But Joshua does not have this advantage.

Nor is Joshua's complaint in verse 7 out of line. 'Alas! Lord Yahweh, why have you brought this people over the Jordan

---

[2] John Calvin, *Commentaries on the Book of Joshua,* trans. Henry Beveridge, in vol. 4 of *Calvin's Commentaries,* 22 vols. (reprint ed.; Grand Rapids: Baker, 1981), 105. The blindness reflected in the scouting report and in Joshua's procedure 'is itself already the first outworking of divine opposition' (Karl Gutbrod, *Das Buch vom Lande Gottes,* Die Botschaft des Alten Testaments, 3d ed. [Stuttgart: Calwer, 1965], 62).

[3] Matthew Henry, *Commentary on the Whole Bible,* 6 vols. (New York: Revell, n.d.), 2:36.

to give us into the hand of the Amorites to destroy us? Oh that we had been content to stay on the other side of the Jordan!' This complaint is different from Israel's unbelieving complaints during the wilderness wanderings (Num. 14:1-3; Deut. 1:27ff.). These are words of despair, not unbelief. Joshua complains to God in prayer; complaining to God is not the same as complaining about God (Israel's wilderness practice).

In his perplexity Joshua makes one basic appeal in his prayer (v. 9). His argument involves the peril of Israel and the honour of Yahweh. Israel's foes, Joshua prays, will cut off 'our name' and then what will you do for 'your great name'? If Israel perishes it will reflect on Yahweh's reputation. So-called re-fined Christians sometimes cringe at the thought of using such arguments in prayer. It seems so crass, they say. (Or does it merely seem too unsophisticated and childlike?) In any case, Matthew Henry is right: 'We cannot urge a better plea than this, Lord, "what wilt thou do for thy great name?' Let God in all be glorified, and then welcome his whole will.'[4] There are times when the people of God today stand in solidarity with Joshua's Israel; that is, there are periods in which confusion strikes and we haven't any idea what God is about. We have no recourse but Joshua's – anguished prayer to a mystifying God, pleading both our danger and his honour.

The Objects of Yahweh's Wrath
Before going further we should consider the objects of Yahweh's wrath. Joshua 7 contains very important teaching about corporate solidarity in sin and judgment.

Immediately, verse 1 presents the interplay between the one and the many: 'the *sons of Israel* committed treachery ... *Achan* took ... so that Yahweh's wrath was hot against the *sons of Israel*'. Again, in verse 11 Yahweh reveals that '*Israel* has sinned', '*they* have transgressed my covenant', whereas in verse 15 he insists that the offender be burned with fire 'because *he* has transgressed the covenant of Yahweh'. Moreover, verses 24-25 make it clear that Achan's family and livestock shared his punishment.[5]

---

[4] Ibid., 2:37.

[5] Observe the fluctuation between 'your fathers' and 'you' (the present generation) in Joshua 24:6-7.

I suppose many twentieth-century American individualists might believe this is unfair. Naturally, we can complain. But we do better to fear. Fear because one man's sin turned away God's presence from a whole people. Fear because a man's whole household was drawn into his punishment. We Christians generally have such tame views of sin; wrongly, we have no paranoia over this contagious power (cf. 1 Cor. 5; Acts 5:1-11).[6]

The Threat of Yahweh's Wrath (7:12b)
Fourthly, we see how central the threat of Yahweh's wrath is. Look again at the structure of chapter 7 mapped out at the beginning of this chapter. There one can observe a certain symmetry in the structure of chapter 7; however, verse 12b seems to serve as the hinge of the whole passage, and rightly so. Hardly anything could be more frightening than to hear Yahweh threaten, 'I will be with you no more, unless you destroy the devoted things from among you' (RSV).

Nothing is more crucial than the presence of Yahweh with his people (1:5, 9; 3:7, 10; 4:14; 6:27); it is the sine qua non of their existence (see Exod. 33:15-16). Now it is about to be forfeited (7:12b). Nothing should disturb God's people more than the loss of God himself from among them.

In Israel's present situation, retaining Yahweh's presence will prove a costly affair – 'unless you destroy the devoted

---

[6] Still, someone will ask (and rightly so) why Achan's family was executed with him. One explanation is that they were likely accessories in his guilt; they must have known where Achan had hidden the loot. I tend to take this view (so too, R. J. Rushdoony, *The Institutes of Biblical Law* [Nutley, N. J.: Presbyterian and Reformed, 1973], 269). However, the text does not explicitly report this, nor does this view explain why his oxen, asses, and sheep were wiped out. They surely were not accomplices. Another explanation holds that a man's personality was regarded as extending to his whole house, so that the 'death of Achan alone would not have answered for the crime which he had committed and that consequently, the rest of *him* [that is], his family and property, were also destroyed....They are appurtenances belonging to him in so intimate a way that they must be included' (R. P. Shedd, *Man in Community* [Grand Rapids: Eerdmans, 1964], 16). Some feel there is a rub between Deuteronomy 24:16 and the punishment of Achan's family. We cannot treat this matter here, but compare C. F. Keil, *Joshua, Judges, Ruth,* Biblical Commentary on the Old Testament (1868; reprint ed.; Grand Rapids: Eerdmans, 1950), 82-83; F. R. Fay, *the Book of Joshua,* Lange's Commentary on the Holy Scriptures, in vol. 2, *Numbers–Ruth* (1870; reprint ed.; Grand Rapids: Zondervan, 1960), 79; and J. H. Hertz, *The Pentateuch and Haftorahs,* 2d ed. (London: Soncino, 1966), 852.

things from among you'. Destructive judgment must take place if the presence of God is to remain (see previous chapter, note 7, on the 'devoted things' or 'ban').

Would it be going too far to say that the apparent absence of God in various segments of the church may be due to our unwillingness to purge evil from our midst by the costly exercise of church discipline? I realise that some churches are too vigorous, punitive, and insensitive in the application of discipline. But, generally, the contemporary church errs on the side of laxity. Somehow we find it convenient to forget the patient threats of Jesus (letters to the churches [Rev. 2–3]), the destructive power of the Spirit (Acts 5:1-11), and the direct commands of the apostles (1 Cor. 5:1-13; 2 Thess. 3:6-15). True, the church does not exist in a theocratic form; hence, it does not execute death penalties. The necessity of discipline, however, does not cease because the form of exercising it has altered. Our problem is that we prefer the tolerance of men to the praise of God.

The Revelation of Yahweh's Wrath (7:10-15)
Nevertheless, in wrath Yahweh remembers mercy, a mercy visible in the revelation of Yahweh's wrath. God does not allow Joshua and Israel to grope in the dark but reveals to them the cause of his displeasure. 'Israel has sinned; ... they have taken some of the devoted things' (v. 11). Behind such unwelcome disclosure shines the clear desire of God to restore his people to his favour. This is the same God who, later, will send Nathan to murdering, adulterous King David (2 Sam. 12:1). Why? Because he refuses to allow his servant to remain comfortable in his sin. He will make it plain to him so that restoration may take place.

The Severity of Yahweh's Wrath (7:16-26)
Now let us come back to the severity of Yahweh's wrath. Not merely Achan but his family, livestock, and possessions suffered the extreme penalty (vv. 24-25). Such severity will disturb some of us, but we must ask why the severe penalty? 'The one taken with the devoted things will be burned with fire – himself and all he has, because he has transgressed

Yahweh's covenant and because he has committed senseless sin in Israel' (v. 15). This verse clearly shows that the penalty is so severe because the sin is so serious. (The NIV wrongly drops the causal particle, 'for/because', and obscures the connection.) The severity of the judgment is an index to the enormity of the sin. Our problem here is – sinners that we are – we don't think breaking Yahweh's covenant is all that big a deal. We really cannot understand God's wrath because sin does not bother us much. That's why we are mystified when we read passages like Exodus 32:25-29 or Numbers 25. That's why we cannot understand Jesus when he tells us we should be willing to go to any extreme to avoid sin (Matt. 5:29-30). It is baffling to us because we do not share Jesus' alarm over sin. The testimony of Joshua 7 is that we cannot treat cancer with vitamin pills; it requires radical surgery. We may think cancer is not that big a deal, but that does not alter God's estimate.

Likely this story was meant to impress Israel with Yahweh's hot wrath against deliberate rebellion. For a lasting monument remains, says the writer – the heap of stones over Achan and Co. (v. 26). And the name of the place, Achor (trouble), a kind of word-play on Achan's name, would call to mind the story (vv. 25-26). In the flow of salvation history one finds monuments to God's saving help (4:1-10) and to his destroying wrath (7:25-26). God's people will pay heed to both of them. They must realise, however, that their God has this way of turning the Valley of Trouble (Achor) into a Door of Hope (Hos. 2:14-15)!

STUDY QUESTIONS:

1. What was the cause of God's wrath with Israel? Could this happen to you?

2. Have you ever prayed to God pleading your danger and his honor? What drove you to that kind of praying?

3. No one sins in isolation. How might your sins affect others?

4. How does the church tolerate sin rather than demand the honor of God?

5. Why do believers think that it is not that big a deal to break God's covenant?

7

Combat and Covenant
(Joshua 8)

Let us begin with some housekeeping chores, that is, problem areas of chapter 8 that we should at least notice.

First, there is the problem of the location of Ai. Most identify biblical Ai with the present site of et-Tell, which is about two miles southeast of modern Beitin (thought to be biblical Bethel). However, archaeological excavations show that et-Tell was uninhabited between circa 2200–1200 BC. This means that whether Israel entered the land around 1400 BC (what is called the 'early date' of the conquest) or approximately 1200 BC (the 'late date'), in either case there was no Ai to conquer; that is, if Ai = et-Tell. In the Early Bronze Age, et-Tell was a city covering twenty-seven acres with a massive stone wall twenty-five feet wide and twenty-nine feet high. Then there was a long gap in occupation. Sometime after 1200 BC there was a small Iron Age I settlement at et-Tell covering three acres.

There appears, however, to be reason to question the usual identification of Ai with et-Tell, because et-Tell is a very large site, while Joshua 7:3 makes the people of Ai 'few' (assuming the spies' report was accurate); et-Tell was not a ruin-heap in the post-conquest period, whereas Joshua 8:28 states that Ai was; and et-Tell does not easily fit the topographical information that the Bible furnishes for Ai (e.g. the mountain between Bethel and Ai [Gen. 12:8]).[1] More light is required before we can positively identify biblical Ai.

A second problem involves the ambush troops. Did Joshua set one or two ambushes (vv. 3ff., 12)? Some prefer to view the 30,000 of verse 3 as specifying the total number of troops used and the 5,000 of verse 12 as indicating the number actually used in the ambush.[2] Though one can read the Hebrew text this way, I do not think it is the more natural view. It seems preferable (even if baffling) to think of two ambush groups of 30,000 and 5,000 respectively. Perhaps Joshua intended one unit to send Ai up in smoke (v. 8) and the other to stifle any further assistance from Bethel (cf. v. 17). On this view Joshua and the main army would be on the north of Ai with two ambush units hidden out to the west of Ai, between Bethel and Ai.[3]

The Definite Help of God (8:1-2)

Now to the teaching of the chapter. Observe how the text highlights the definite help of God (especially vv. 1-2). This point is clear from the structure of verses 1-29:

Reassurance from Yahweh, 1-2
   Instructions to the ambush, 3-9
      Joshua and all Israel go up, 10-13
         'Victory' of Ai, 14-17
Direction from Yahweh, 18
   Action of the ambush, 19-20
      Joshua and all Israel turn back, 21-23
         Defeat of Ai, 24-27
         (Summary, 28-29)

---

[1] See H. G. Stigers, *A Commentary on Genesis* (Grand Rapids: Zondervan, 1976), 140; Jehushua M. Grintz, ' 'Ai Which Is Beside Beth-Aven', *Biblica* 42 (1961): 201-16; and John J. Bimson, *Redating the Exodus and Conquest,* Journal for the Study of the Old Testament/Supplement Series 5 (Sheffield, 1978), 215-25.

[2] E.g. George Bush, *Notes, Critical and Practical, on the Book of Joshua* (Chicago: Henry A. Sumner, 1881), 89-90.

[3] On the problem of large numbers (e.g. 30,000), see the discussion in William S. LaSor, David A. Hubbard, and Frederic W. Bush, *Old Testament Survey: The Message, Form, and Background of the Old Testament* (Grand Rapids: Eerdmans, 1982), 166-70.

The structure of these verses is quite symmetrical; it is important to notice that at the head of both major segments stands Yahweh's reassurance and instruction for the assault on Ai (vv. 1-2, 18). The reassurance of verse 1 resembles that given prior to Jericho (6:2). Yahweh is in such control that he specifies the precise moment for the counterattack (v. 18). Even the ambush is no bright idea of Joshua or Israel but part of Yahweh's instructions (v. 2) There's a conspiracy in the text: to show that the 'all-surpassing power is from God and not from us' (2. Cor. 4:7, NIV). Even the cleverness is his!

Bear in mind the timing and necessity of Yahweh's help. It comes after sin has been dealt with and judgment executed (ch. 7). (For commentary, see Isaiah 59:1-2.) Israel must have God's power for even little Ai (assuming the spy report given in 7:3 was accurate). With the power of God the great Jericho could be taken (ch. 6); without his power not even the smallest post could be overrun.[4] How utterly dependent God's people are upon God's power for any success! This is what the text preaches to us.[5]

The Generous Gifts of God (8:2, 27)

Secondly, this passage points us to the generous gifts of God. In contrast to the episode at Jericho (6:18, 21), Yahweh here allows Israel to take Ai's 'spoil and its livestock' for themselves (v. 2). There had been precedent for this (Deut. 2:34-35). How needless Achan's covetousness was (7:21)! When Yahweh's priority is recognised and satisfied (6:18-19), he then gives to his people. God never seeks to impoverish his people. It is only as his people lose sight of his generosity, his provision, his goodness, that the cancer of covetousness consumes them. Indeed this is one of the first principles of 'serpent theology', for the tempter was sharp enough to place his emphasis on the restriction God has imposed rather than on the riches he had lavished (Gen. 3:1). Recognising Yahweh as the giving God

---

[4] See Karl Gutbrod, *Das Buch vom Lande gottes,* Die Botschaft des Alten Testaments, 3d ed. (Stuttgart: Calwer, 1965), 72.

[5] One may see a parallel between Joshua's javelin here (vv. 18-19, 26) and Moses' rod in Exodus 17. On the latter see Willem Hendrik Gispen, *Exodus*, The Bible Student's Commentary (Grand Rapids: Zondervan, 1982), 166, 168-71.

is the prerequisite for faithfulness; contentment with God's goodness is our antidote for apostasy.

The Solemn Judgment of God (8:29)

Third, what a picture we have of the solemn judgment of God. 'But the king of Ai [Joshua] hung on a tree until evening time; and as the sun was going down Joshua gave command and they took his body down from the tree, threw it into the opening of the city gate, and raised over him a high heap of stones – until this day.'

Contemporary Bible readers often cringe in the face of such descriptions, conjuring up thoughts of that 'barbaric' age. (Actually, it is our century that has the corner on barbarism, while the Old Testament is, comparatively speaking, rather clean.) But our superficial reactions must not blind us to what the text describes as a solemn and significant matter.

Such hangings will occur later (10:26-27) and probably occurred at Jericho (cf. v. 2). The hanging, however, was not the means of death but a sequel to death. Kings were hung after they had been put to death (see again 10:26-27). The law of Deuteronomy 21:22-23 gives us some help here. An Israelite offender put to death for a capital offence could then be hung up on a tree or post, probably to 'serve as a warning to the population of the results of breaking those laws which were punishable by death'.[6] But the corpse was to be taken down before nightfall. There is a significant statement in these provisions: 'Any one who is hung on a tree is under God's curse' (Deut. 21:23, niv). P. C. Craigie has stated the matter well:

> The body was not 'accursed of God' ... because it was hanging on a tree; it was hanging on a tree because it was accursed of God. And the body was not accursed of God simply because it was dead (for all men die), but it was accursed because of the reason [crime against God's law] for the death.[7]

The hanging of the king of Ai is probably to be viewed in this light. Here is a solemn sign that he and his people (in fact,

[6] P. C. Craigie, *The Book of Deuteronomy*, The New International Commentary on the Old Testament (Grand Rapids: Eerdmans, 1976), 285.
[7] Ibid.

all Canaan) stand under Yahweh's curse and judgment. Why? See Leviticus 18:24-25 and Deuteronomy 9:4-5. Certainly, it is gruesome. But perhaps the living God must stoop to such spectacles; else we might never fear sin. Even at this moment you and I may not be overwhelmed by the gravity of God's judgment – it is only something that happened to the king of Ai back in 1400 BC. Yet for the hardness of our hearts God has given us still another picture of his judgment – the King of the Jews hanging on a tree, 'having become a curse for us' (Gal. 3:13). Perhaps we will not take that so lightly. Perhaps we will not say that is only something that happened back in AD 30.

The Artistic Praise of God

Before considering verses 30-35, we should make an observation regarding the style of the whole chapter (something we could point out frequently); the way the story is told reflects the artistic praise of God.

This story of Ai's defeat was told in praise of Yahweh. We don't always think this way when reading biblical narratives, but we should. This story, no less than Psalm 100, declares Yahweh's praise. Here Israel praises her God for mighty help against her adversaries at Ai.

The story is not mere praise, however, but well-constructed praise. The ambush is, as previously stated, Yahweh's command; it is not a clever thought of Israel. But observe how the ambush is merely mentioned in verse 2. No details are given. Next, Joshua spells out some details in verses 3-9. For example, when Joshua and men draw Ai's defenders away, the ambushers are to take the city and set it on fire (vv. 7-8). That's all. Then in the report of the actual attack in verses 20-26 we are told that Ai's forces were caught between the ambushers and Joshua's counterattack.

This is good storytelling. Think what would have happened to our interest if the writer had included all this information at the first. If he had included in the Lord's instructions not merely the mention of the ambush but directions for taking and firing the city and for coming out of the city and striking at the rear of Ai's troops, why, we would have known all from the start. There would have been no suspense, no curiosity as to what would happen next. Our writer narrates the praise of God but is careful to keep it interesting at the same time. A good model for us.

Several years ago I was traveling a highway in a state where we used to live. There was a well-advertised roadside fruit stand along this highway, but some of its signs read 'Larry's Fruiet Stand'. Naturally, I inferred that 'fruiet' was identical with 'fruit'. But someone of more critical ilk might see that sign and think, 'Why, if they can't even spell "fruit" correctly, I wonder what sort of joint it is?' Larry probably has splendid fruit, but his 'packaging' should commend rather than demean his product.

The writer of Joshua knew this. He rehearsed the praise of Yahweh in 8:1-29, yet did it in a careful and interesting way. There is surely some carryover for us. Our public worship need not be jazzy, but neither should it be joyless, tedious, and routinely predictable. Not if we worship the God of the Bible. Perhaps our preaching should not be racy and sensational, but neither should it be dull, lifeless, and unexciting. If we really have a fascinating God, then that fascination and wonder will spill over in the way we speak to him and of him.

The Crucial Word of God (8:30-35)
Finally, we must spend some time on verses 30-35, for here we see the crucial word of God.

At 8:30-35 an abrupt shift occurs. In 8:29 we were standing at the gate of Ai watching its king receive the last rites. Now – verse 30 – we have been whisked away and find ourselves in the shadow of Mount Ebal near Shechem hearing the blessing and curse of the Torah (Law). Suddenly, we are more than twenty miles north of Ai. This sudden transition has caused some to question whether verses 30-35 really belong here.[8] J. Alberto Soggin claims verses 30-35 'have no link with what

---

[8] The Septuagint (a Greek translation of the Old Testament, dating from circa 200 BC and later, usually abbreviated LXX) places 8:30-35 after 9:2. But the Septuagint has wrongly done so, for it thereby destroys the contrast that the traditional Hebrew text (MT = Massoretic Text) intends between the reaction of the kings in 9:1-2 and that of the Gibeonites in 9:3; this last should be translated adversatively ('But the residents of Gibeon...').

precedes them nor with what follows' and admits that it is 'not at all clear why 8:30-35 have been put in their present context'.[9]

But this is a superficial view. First, 8:30-35 is perfectly in place if one considers the overall structure of chapters 5–8:

Heading, 5:1 (cf. 9:1; 10:1; 11:1)
Preparation: Covenant sacraments, 5:2-12
Onslaught
   Firstfruits, 5:13–6:27 (success); war of Yahweh
   Curse, 7:1-26 (failure); anger of Yahweh
   Restoration, 8:1-29 (success); help of Yahweh
Conclusion: Covenant word, 8:30-35

Looking at this overview, we see that 8:30-35 is simply the end piece that corresponds to 5:2-12. We cannot extensively discuss this. Suffice it to say that chapters 5–8 appear to be a carefully constructed block of material and that the reading of the covenant law (8:30-35) appropriately closes off a large section introduced by participation in the covenant signs (circumcision and Passover [5:2-12]).

Secondly, there is a clear thematic link between 8:30-35 and the preceding material. After Israel had just experienced the curse of Yahweh's anger (ch. 7) and the boon of Yahweh's aid (ch. 8), what could be more appropriate than Joshua's reading 'the blessing and the curse' (v. 34) of the Torah?

Having said this, one must still confess that 8:30-35 does give us a literary jolt. We have been accustomed to reading a fairly continuous narrative of strategies and battles when, suddenly, the war movie is cut and we are left looking at a slide of a worship service. We are wrenched from conquest to covenant.[10] The situation is like the interruption of normal television programming with a special news bulletin. The news bulletin is deemed of sufficient importance and priority

---

[9] J. Alberto Soggin, *Joshua: A Commentary*, Old Testament Library (Philadelphia: Westminster, 1972), 241.

[10] If 8:30-35 is in precise chronological order with the surrounding narrative, it shows that Israel deliberately made the trek from Ai to Shechem, since after the victory at Ai (9:3) Israel went back to camp at Gilgal (9:6) near the Jordan.

to preempt normal telecasting. That is why the biblical writer makes us victims of his literary violence: to underscore the fact that covenant obedience has priority over military victory (indeed, that the former is the basis of the latter – remember ch. 7); to show that heeding God's word is more crucial than fighting God's war. By placing this covenant renewal ceremony here, the writer is saying that Israel's success does not primarily consist in knocking off Canaanites but in everyone's total submission to the word of God. It is as if he is saying, 'Stop the war and listen to the law of God; this is the most urgent matter right now.' (See Deut. 11:29-32 and 27:1-14, where Moses commanded Israel to carry out this ceremony.)

The climax of the ceremony comes with Joshua's reading (or proclaiming) all the words of the law (vv. 34-35). Notice how the text emphasises that all the word was applicable to all the people ('all' is used five times in vv. 33-35). The sojourner as well as the native Israelite, leaders as well as rank-and-file Israelites are to be ruled by this word. This law is not merely some official record for the archives but a lively, personal word for shaping the lives of housewives, kids, and hangers-on (see v. 35b). All the people of God must give all obedience to all the word of God. This is Israel's first priority.

What we have just said about the ceremony at Shechem has stressed that it constituted a demand upon the people of Yahweh; but we should also point out that it served as a witness to the faithfulness of Yahweh. It is significant that this covenant ceremony was to be held at Shechem (where Mount Ebal and Mount Gerazim were located; about forty miles north of Jerusalem). Here Abram (Abraham) had first received the promise of the land (Gen. 12:6-7). Here Jacob had returned safely after a long exile from the land he had been promised (Gen. 33:18-20; 28:13). And now, in Joshua 8, here is Abraham's seed, here is Jacob's family, at Promise Place, experiencing the fulfilment of Yahweh's promise of the land. Surely our writer wants us to note the significance of the location; it is a way of recognising the faithfulness of God. It is his way of saying that time does not invalidate Yahweh's promises.

STUDY QUESTIONS:

1. What are the 'little' things that you are tempted to leave God out of, thinking that you can handle it yourself?

2. In what ways have you seen 'serpent theology' in the life of the church?

3. How does the dictum of "cursed is any one hanging on a tree" relate to the death of Christ? Does the 'tree' bring the curse or does the 'curse' bring the tree?

4. How might you 'dull' the message of God's grace rather than proclaim its wonder?

5. In what ways has God caused you to pause from your 'work' and to look at His word? Why is such renewal important?

8

The Trouble with Common Sense
(Joshua 9)

Our chapter deals with the trickery of the Gibeonites in foxing Israel into a treaty. When discussing chapter 10 we will want to note the location of Gibeon and satellite towns and the broader structure of chapters 9–12. For the present, let us focus on 9:3-27. The structure and content of the story are as follows:

Gibeon's reaction to Israel's conquest, 3-15
    Preparing provisions, 4-5
      Request for covenant, 6-8
      (Israel cautious)
        'Confession' about Yahweh, 9-11
    Displaying provisions, 12-13
      Cutting of covenant, 14-15
      (Israel deceived)
Israel's reaction to Gibeon's deceit, 16-27
    Deliverance of Gibeon, 18-21
      Dealing with Israel: the oath is sacred
        The oath and the complaint of the people, 18
        The oath and the answer to the complaint, 19-21
    Doom of Gibeon, 22-25
      Dealing with Gibeon: the curse is perpetual

The delegation from Gibeon (located about six miles north-west of Jerusalem) arrives in Israel's camp at Gilgal near Jericho and the Jordan. Strange that their deception so closely follows the dedication of 8:30-35. The Gibeonites are moved not only by news of Israel's victories but also by certain knowledge they have about Israel's designs and policy. They seemed to know that Israel was directed to dispossess and exterminate the residents of Canaan and probably knew that Israel was to make no treaties with these peoples (v. 24; see Exod. 23:31-33; 34:12; Deut. 7:2). But they may also have known that Israel was permitted to spare and conclude peace with cities located 'very far from you' (see Deut. 20:10-18); doubtless for this reason the Gibeonites stress that they are from 'a distant land' (vv. 6, 9).

The Lack of the Wisdom of God (9:3-15)
First of all, this story means to impress us with how Israel suffers from the lack of the wisdom of God.

How Israel needed wisdom, for the Gibeonites come with such tangible evidence (vv. 4-5, 12-13). Everything is worn out – grain sacks, wineskins, sandals, clothes. Their bread is dry and crusty. It is much like watching a television commercial about some leading anti-acid that soaks up much more excess stomach acid than its competitor. There is no way to prove its claims, but it seems convincing because of this demonstration. Two beakers are filled with liquid, equivalent, I suppose, to stomach fluid and – sure enough – the one anti-acid shows itself markedly superior to the other. Now that is not really convincing proof at all, but it appears credible because of this visible, tangible, so-called scientific demonstration. It conveys the impression of solid evidence. So it is with Israel. Who could dispute the obvious except with divine insight?

The Gibeonites also offer a realistic report (vv. 9-10). What moved them, they say, was hearing what Yahweh had done in Egypt and how he had wiped out Sihon and Og on the eastern side of the Jordan (on the latter, see Num. 21:21-35). What really moved Gibeon was what Joshua had done to Jericho and Ai (v. 3). But, craftily (v. 4), they don't mention Jericho or Ai to Joshua. After all, they are from a 'very distant land' (v. 9) and so couldn't possibly have heard of these latest developments! In a very distant land they could be expected to know the old, old story but hardly the latest news.

Perhaps the most deceptive of all was the spiritual testimony they offered (vv. 9-11). It was the reputation of Yahweh earned in his mighty acts that drew them to come, so they say. One might compare their words with Rahab's confession of faith in 2:10-13. How difficult to tell the difference between faith (like Rahab's) and flattery (like Gibeon's), especially when that flattery is so spiritual and pious. It is all very subtle because 'there is always something heart-warming for most of us when we hear that God's dealings with us are being spoken of by people at a distance'.[1]

How Israel needed wisdom, yet how Israel neglected wisdom! Whether verse 14a alludes to participating in a covenant meal is not so crucial. We catch the main concern when we hear verse 14b bemoaning Israel's folly: 'but the mouth of Yahweh they did not ask' ('the mouth of Yahweh' carries the emphasis in the Hebrew text). Joshua and his men should have inquired of Yahweh through Eleazar the priest (see Num. 27:21). Yahweh's direction was available but was ignored.

Now it was not that Joshua and the elders did not ask the right questions; they were suspicious at just the right points (vv. 7-8). It was not that they were sloppy in their investigation but that they were alone in their decision. It wasn't that they didn't think but that they didn't pray. They did not have because they did not ask (James 4:2).

This episode raises pertinent questions for God's people. Do we need the guidance of God only when we are in doubt? Do we not need to be careful when we begin to think, 'There is no need to consult the Lord on this matter – it's quite clear'? 'No

---

[1] H. L. Ellison, *Scripture Union Bible Study Books: Joshua – 2 Samuel* (Grand Rapids: Eerdmans, 1966), 10.

proposed course of conduct can be so clear to a Christian as to excuse him from the duty of seeking direction from above.'[2] Not that you have to ask the Lord whether you should get a haircut at four o'clock. The Scriptures do not require wilting in the everlasting arms, only leaning on them. But we must beware of that subtle unbelief that assumes 'I have this under control.'

I was eight or ten years old and playing in the back yard of an older boy who lived across the street. He had gone in to eat supper and I was left to play in his back yard with my baseball bat and ball until he could return. As I stood facing his house with bat on my shoulder and ball in my hand, I noticed the door that led to the family's basement. There was a window in it. Suddenly the thought occurred to me that it would be extremely unlikely for me to hit my ball from 100 feet away and smash that window in the basement door. Well do I remember how in control I felt about that. And just to prove my point I decided to try breaking that window by hitting my ball. Well, I was right, but I was not in control. I did not break the basement window; I smashed the kitchen window where the family was eating supper! Yet I still recall that psychological feeling I had before the deed – 'I can handle this.'

Joshua 9 warns God's people against such cocky independence. In the context of our various trials we need wisdom to know how to function in those trials and circumstances; it is available from a giving God, and we are to ask for it (James 1:5). Our need is no different from Israel's. We need not only the power of God to overwhelm our obvious enemies but also the wisdom of God to detect our subtle enemies. Unfortunately, the church too often craves God's power while it ignores God's wisdom.

The Concern over the Honour of God (9:16-21)

Secondly, our chapter portrays the concern over the honour of God. Soon Israel discovers the Gibeonites live nearby; Israel has been tricked into an oath. And the whole dilemma centres around the oath 'we have sworn' (vv. 18, 19, 20). The people

---

[2] George Bush, *Notes, Critical and Practical, on the Book of Joshua* (Chicago: Henry A. Summer, 1881), 105.

of Israel are upset with their leaders (v. 18b); the people probably reasoned that an oath obtained by deceit need not be honoured (cf. v. 19).[3] However, the leaders seem to be swayed by other considerations: to break the oath (even though it was wrongly obtained) would bring Yahweh's wrath upon Israel (as he executed the curse for breaking a covenant oath); to break the oath would dishonour the name of Yahweh before the pagans (vv. 19-20; they had sworn 'by Yahweh the God of Israel' and any breach of such oath implies that Yahweh cannot be trusted). Hence the Gibeonites are to become woodcutters and water carriers for Israel's sanctuary (v. 21).

Naturally, we Christians in the West have a difficult time understanding why Israel sticks to this oath. That is because we have such a low view of the given word and such a flimsy concern for truth (Ps. 15:4; Matt. 23:16-22).

Israel was stuck. They must not break an oath, though it had been wrongly obtained, because they had wrongly neglected the wisdom of God. What to do? Live as faithfully as they could within that twisted situation.

This demand spills over into Christian experience. Sometimes God's people are called to live obediently amidst the results of their folly. There are times when our preferences, our conveniences, our justifications must not be allowed to dissolve those difficult situations.

Three or four years ago our oldest son made a bet with a fellow sixth-grader on the National League (baseball) play-offs. The bet was for $3 and our son lost! Now my boy knew he was not allowed to bet. (In my view, betting, which assumes chance, is a tacit denial of the sovereignty of God.) Yet he did it – and lost. What he had done was wrong, yet he had given his word. So I told him he would have to pay. All his resources, $2.41, plus 59¢ from Dad, were taken to school for the pay-off. Happily, the other father would not allow his son to take the money!

You may question my attempts at child-rearing. But I'm concerned for the principle, not the particulars. We may be

---

[3] A number of interpreters would agree. See F. R. Fay, *The Book of Joshua*, Lange's Commentary on the Holy Scriptures, in vol. 2, *Numbers–Ruth* (1870; reprint ed.; Grand Rapids: Zondervan, 1960), 90-91.

caught in a framework of our sin, wrong, and folly. Surely we need repentance and forgiveness – yet eradication of guilt does not eliminate all the consequences of sin. We must, therefore, be faithful to God in the wake of our mistakes and be assured that his mercy does not cease because we have been wrong. We must glorify and magnify the grace of God in our messes.

The Hope Under the People of God (9:22-27)

Lastly, this chapter may point to the hope under the people of God. Here I may be pressing beyond the text and so ask the reader to use discernment.

The Gibeonites escaped with their lives (cf. vv. 24, 26) but lived under a curse (v. 23). They were woodcutters and water carriers for Yahweh's sanctuary (v. 27). Sheer drudgery was to be their lot. Yet one might detect a redemptive hint here.

> They were hereby brought into a situation where they would naturally acquire the knowledge of the true God and of his revealed will, were made to dwell in the courts of the Lord's house, were honored with near access to him in the services of the sanctuary, and thus placed in circumstances eminently favorable to their spiritual and eternal interests.[4]

This suggestion would appear to be a legitimate inference from the text. I am not completely sure the text intends to imply this. But I would not be surprised if it did, for it is so like the God of which it speaks, who brings light out of darkness, hope out of despair, gladness out of mourning, grace out of cursing.

Study Questions:

1. Have you ever been fooled by the 'spiritual testimony' of someone? How did you come to realize the 'untruth'?

---

[4] Bush, *Joshua*, 108. The reader may find a similar view in Matthew Henry, *Commentary on the Whole Bible*, 6 vols. (New York: Revell, n.d.), 2:55, and in Hugh J. Blair, 'Joshua', in *The New Bible Commentary: Revised* (Grand Rapids: Eerdmans, 1970), 243.

2. When are you most tempted to handle things yourself rather than seeking wisdom or prayer?

3. Do you need the wisdom of God only when you are in doubt?

4. Some might call Israel's oath keeping 'eating crow.' When has your own folly lead to such crow-eating diners?

5. Do you think that there is a redemptive focus here concerning the Gibeonites? If so, how might you be a blessing to non-believers in common places?

9

In Canaan's Dixie
(Joshua 10)

Joshua 9–11 forms a fairly connected unit. We may briefly summarise it as follows:

Israel without Yahweh, 9:1-27
Yahweh with Israel, 10:1–11:15
    Southern campaign, 10:1-43
        Setting, 10:1-5
        Summary, 10:40-43
    Northern campaign, 11:1-15
        Setting, 11:1-5
        Summary, 11:12-15
Summary, 11:16-23

Joshua 10 focuses on Israel's success down in Canaan's Dixie, Israel's southern campaign. However, before discussing chapter 10 itself, geography merits our attention.

We can appreciate Adoni-zedek's dismay (10:1-2) once we observe the strategic location of the Gibeonite 'tetrapolis' (9:17). The four towns, Gibeon, Chephirah, Beeroth, and Kiriath-jearim, constituted a confederation of which Gibeon was apparently the dominant participant. Gibeon (if it is el-Jib[1]) was six miles north/northwest of Jerusalem, guarded the eastern end of the 'way of Beth-horon' (an important road between Jerusalem and Ajalon to the west), and was a junction for local roads. Chephirah was five miles west of Gibeon on a spur of a plateau where it commanded approaches to Gibeon from the west. Kiriath-jearim stood two miles south of Chephirah, six miles southwest of Gibeon, situated on the road from Judah to Beth-Shemesh and Timnah, sites in the Sorek Valley. No one knows where Beeroth was: perhaps near Khirbet el-Burj, about two miles south of Gibeon (el-Jib).[2]

Why should Adoni-zedek be so upset from looking at his map of the holy land? Because he knew that Israel had already knocked off Jericho and Ai to the east. Now the Gibeonite confederation in the centre and west had concluded peace with Israel. Here was a rectangle of four key sites now under Joshua's control. Along with Israel's defeat of Jericho and Ai, this meant that Israel had control of the strategic central plateau (later to belong to the tribe of Benjamin); Joshua had cut a swath right across the midsection of Canaan.[3] He had driven a wedge between north and south.

The Warrior of Israel (10:8-11)

Turning to the chapter's teaching, we see in verses 8-11 a picture of Yahweh as the warrior of Israel. Adoni-zedek had sent for his cronies to come up and help him smash Gibeon (vv. 3-5); the Gibeonites had sent for Joshua to come up and help them get relief from these Amorite kings (vv. 6-7).

At this point let us pause to note a couple of instructive items in verses 8-9. In verse 8 Yahweh assures Joshua: 'Do not be afraid of them, for I have given them into your hand; not one of them will stand before you.' The latter part of this assurance had already been given to Joshua in 1:5 before the invasion of Canaan. Now Yahweh repeats it. Such is the usual way God

[1] The jar handles inscribed 'Gibeon' found at el-Jib do not necessarily prove el-Jib is biblical Gibeon. See J. Simons, *The Geographical and Topographical Texts of the Old Testament* (Leiden: E. J. Brill, 1959), 176.

[2] On Beeroth see Anson F. Rainey, 'Beeroth', *IDB/S*, 93; also Trent C. Butler, *Joshua*, Word Biblical Commentary (Waco: Word, 1983), 103.

[3] For the geography of Joshua the reader will find a helpful series of maps in John Lilley, 'Joshua', in *The New Layman's Bible Commentary* (Grand Rapids: Zondervan, 1979), 315-33.

has of reassuring his children: not by unveiling to them some new truth previously unknown, but by reaffirming promises already given, which somehow take on special power because of the present pressing need. That is what God's people usually need – not new truth but old truth freshly applied to their current need.

Then note that verse 9 shows how divine reassurance (v. 8) does not stifle but stimulates human ingenuity (the surprise attack), how God's comfort does not sedate but calls forth his servant's activity. Yahweh has promised victory (v. 8), but his victory will be achieved through a forced night march and a surprise attack, probably while still dark (v. 9). The truth of God's sovereignty, rightly used, does not enervate but energises human response.

The picture of Yahweh as warrior appears in verses 10-11. We find a good deal of variety here in the English translations of verse 10. There are four verbs in verse 10. Yahweh is expressly the subject of the first verb ('threw [them] into panic'). The Revised Standard Version, New International Version, and Today's English Version make Israel the subject of the next three verbs (NEB votes for Joshua), though the American Standard Version, New American Standard Bible, and Jerusalem Bible take Yahweh as subject of these verbs as well. The traditional Hebrew text assumes Yahweh is the subject of all four verbs.[4] I think this is what the writer intended. Granted, it may sound strange to us to hear of Yahweh pursuing, for example, the enemy. But that is precisely the point; the writer wants us to see that it is Yahweh who is the fighter; he is the warrior, he is the victor who crushes the enemy. As if to italicise this truth, verse 11 states that '*Yahweh* [emphatic in the Hebrew] threw down great stones from heaven' upon the enemy. More perished by Yahweh's hail than by Israel's sword (v. 11b). The text is declaring the source and cause of Israel's victory. Yahweh is the warrior who defeats the foe; Israel must not miss this.

It is too bad much of the church has lost this vision of God or Christ as the warrior who fights for his people. Too many of

---

[4] The Septuagint takes Yahweh as the subject of the first two verbs and Israel (understood) as the subject of the second two.

us regard this conception as substandard, by which we mean it does not fit our sentimental twentieth-century graven images of what God ought to be like. The imagery seems too violent. And we do the same for the Lord Jesus, with perhaps not a little help from church school materials. The popular image of Jesus is that he is not only kind and tender but also soft and prissy, as though Jesus comes to us reeking of hand cream. Such a Jesus can hardly steel the soul that is daily assaulted by the enemy. We need to learn the catechism of Psalm 24. Question: Who is the King of glory? Answer: Yahweh, strong and mighty! Yahweh – mighty in battle! (Ps. 24:8). We must catch the vision of the Faithful and True sitting on the white horse, the One who 'judges and makes war' in righteousness (Rev. 19:11-16). No mild God or soft Jesus can give his people hope. It is only as we know the warrior of Israel who fights for us (and sometimes without us) that we have hope of triumphing in the muck of life.

The Miracle of Prayer (10:12-14)
Secondly, we meet the miracle of prayer. Please note this main point. That is the emphasis in the text. However, there are some questions to be clarified before we focus on this major thrust.

I hold that the text means to describe a historical occurrence. But for what did Joshua ask? The more common view is that he asked for an extension of daylight so that Israel could make the most of its victory. Others, however, hold that he was likely asking for an extension of darkness for the same reason. Let us consider this question through a discussion of the 'darkness view', since it is not so widely known.

The darkness position is not so outlandish as it may seem when one considers questions of translation and context. In verse 12b most versions indicate Joshua commanded the sun and moon to 'stand still'. The Hebrew verb (*damam*) means to be dumb, silent, or still. That is general enough. The question too seldom asked is: Which activity of sun and moon is Joshua prohibiting? Most assume it is their movement. But why could it not be their shining? The latter makes sense in the context, since Joshua had marched all night and made a sudden attack

(v. 9), which likely means he made the attack while it was still dark. Moreover, Joshua's 'sun command' assumes that the sun was to the east at Gibeon and the moon to the west over Ajalon, which means he spoke in the early morning. That would be an appropriate time to ask for prolonged darkness (i.e. so the troops wouldn't be sapped by the searing heat?) but a bit early to be concerned about an extension of daylight.[5]

But if *damam* could connote 'be silent (from shining)', 'be dark', what about when verse 13a says the moon 'stood' ('stopped', NIV; 'halted', NEB) and verse 13b says the same of the sun? The verb is the very common *'amad* (to stand). But again, is the reference to motion or radiance? The range of *'amad* is broader than 'stand still in a position'; it can denote a mother's ceasing to bear children (Gen. 29:35; 30:9), the sea's ceasing to rage (Jonah 1:15), an archer's ceasing to shoot (2 Kings 13:18), oil ceasing to flow (2 Kings 4:6). In fact, Habakkuk 3:11 seems to use *'amad* of the sun and moon's ceasing to shine, since they were outshined by God's light and, apparently, darkened in the storm.[6]

However, the very last clause of verse 13 poses a major obstacle for the darkness position. That clause notes that the sun 'did not hasten to go down for about a whole day' (RSV). R. D. Wilson averred that a careful examination showed that the last phrase should be translated 'as on a completed (i.e. ordinary) day'.[7] One could argue that if the sun was not visible this clause may well describe how the situation appeared to an observer on terra firma – since the sun was blacked out one could not see it 'run its course' (Ps. 19:5-6) as on an ordinary

---

[5] If Yahweh's hailstorm of verse 11 came chronologically after Joshua's prayer it would likely have been dark. The 'then' of verse 12a does not necessarily indicate temporal sequence, so it is possible that Yahweh's hailstorm was a response to Joshua's prayer. This is how the apocryphal book of Ecclesiasticus (46:5-6) took it.

[6] On Habakkuk 3:11 see Carl E. Armerding, 'Habukkuk', in *The Expositor's Bible Commentary*, ed. Frank E. Gaebelein, 12 vols. (Grand Rapids: Zondervan, 1985), 7:529-30; A. B. Davidson and H. C. O. Lanchester, *The Books of Nahum, Habakkuk and Zephaniah*, Cambridge Bible for Schools and Colleges (Cambridge: The University Press, 1920), 93; cf. also C. F. Keil, *The Twelve Minor Prophets*, Biblical Commentary on the Old Testament (1868; reprint ed.; Grand Rapids: Eerdmans, 1949), 2:108.

[7] R. D. Wilson, 'Understanding "The Sun Stood Still"', in *Classical Evangelical Essays in Old Testament Interpretation*, ed. Walter C. Kaiser, Jr. (Grand Rapids: Baker, 1972), 62 (reprint from *Princetown Theological Review* 16 [1918]: 46-54).

day. However, some will view such a suggestion as an evasion of the difficulty and use it as an opportunity to play 'stone the interpreter'. So I won't press it.

Suffice it to say that, on balance, I prefer the darkness view, because it is more suitable to the context, though, admittedly, the last clause of verse 13 may augur ill for it.[8]

Having bathed in all that ink, let us return to the major stress of the text, the miracle of prayer. The writer observes that 'there has not been a day like that, before or since, when Yahweh listened to the voice of a man, for Yahweh [emphatic] fought for Israel' (v. 14). That day was unique not for some unusual daylight or darkness but because Yahweh listened to a man's prayer!

Granted, it was some prayer! Though it was spoken to Yahweh (v. 12a), it was nevertheless a man's direct command (v. 12b) to elements under only God's control. Yet 'Yahweh listened to the voice of a man.' Astounding! Isn't it still amazing that God listens to the voice of a man or woman who comes to him? Doesn't this view of prayer both rebuke both the flippancy and tedium with which we often approach the Great King? Ought we not catch our breath to think that the God who is seated on high (Ps. 113:5) stoops down and bends his ear to lips of dust and ashes? 'When he calls to me, I will answer him' (Ps.91:15); who ever heard of a God like that?

The Sign of Victory (10:16-27)
In the third place, verses 16-27 focus on the sign of victory. These verses relate the aftermath of the Battle of Beth-Horon (vv. 1-15), while verses 28-43 go on to detail something of the whole southern campaign.[9]

---

[8] For further reading on verses 12-14, see E. W. Maunder, 'Beth-Horon, the Battle of', *ISBE* (rev. ed.), 1:469-71; Bernard Ramm, *The Christian View of Science and Scripture* (Grand Rapids: Eerdmans, 1954), 156-61; and Hugh J. Blair, 'Joshua', in *The New Bible Commentary: Revised* (Grand Rapids: Eerdmans, 1970), 244.

[9] Some scholars have trouble with the fact that the closure of verse 43 also appears at verse 15. Everyone knows, so goes the claim, that Joshua and Israel did not go back to Gilgal (by the Jordan) after verse 14 and then return to south Canaan for further campaigning in verses 16-43. I would hold that the biblical writer also knew as much. I simply take verse 15 as a colophon closing off one section of the story. The story opens up again at verse 16, with the rest of the chapter describing the follow-up of the initial battle as well as offering a synopsis of an extended campaign in the

The five ringleader kings hide in a cave at Makkedah. Israel traps them in, guards the cave, while the rest of the troops make the most of the rout begun at Beth-Horon. When they return to Makkedah, Joshua orders the five kings brought out and Israel's military chiefs to 'come near and put your feet upon the necks of these kings' (v. 24).

Now this act was not simple barbarism nor a mere macho move. It was, if one might speak loosely, a sacrament. Joshua's words in verse 25 explain the action: 'Don't be afraid and don't lose your nerve; be strong and bold, for this is what Yahweh will do to all your enemies with whom you are fighting.' The leaders' feet upon the necks of these prostrate kings was an acted parable, an assuring sign, of how Yahweh would certainly place all their enemies beneath them. The symbolic action is intended as a visible encouragement to the people of God.

Of course, some skeptic may question how a mere symbolic action could ever reassure faith, since there is no compelling logic in it. And one must admit as much. How God's bow in the clouds could make Noah feel the security of God's promise (Gen. 9:11-17) or how scads of stars should elicit Abram's faith in a countless seed (Gen. 15:1-6) – these remain mysteries. Sacraments are not for skeptics but are for believers as props for our weak faith. They are not intended to convince us by cold logic but to nurture us by warm encouragement, to make us *feel* that God's word is reliable and his help sure. Who can explain how eating bread and drinking wine assures us that the crucified and risen Jesus will now and always sustain us? So dirty Israelite feet planted on royal Canaanite necks provide fresh encouragement that 'this is what Yahweh will do to all your enemies'.

---

south of Palestine. Then the more detailed account is closed off by the same formula (v. 43 par. v. 15). Hebrew narrative frequently begins with a summary of an event and continues with an expansion of it in greater detail; or it begins with a somewhat brief account of the main event and follows up by spelling out the aftermath of that event in more detail. I call this the summary-expansion pattern of Hebrew narrative. The reader may check the following examples: Genesis 14:1-4/5-12; 21:22-24/25-32; 37:5/6-8; Exodus 14:1-4/5-30; Numbers 13:1-3/17-20; Joshua 21:4-7/8-40; Judges 4:12-16/17-22; 20:29-36a/36b-48; 1 Samuel 14:6-23 (or, 20-23)/24-46; 2 Samuel 2:12-17/18-32; 18:6-8/9-18. Hence Joshua 10:6-15 and 16-43 follow the same scheme, and there is no need to have cerebral shift over verse 15.

One more note about this. The encouragement Joshua gives in verse 25 is the very same he had received. God had previously ordered Joshua not to 'lose your nerve' (1:9) and had repeatedly commanded him to 'be strong and bold' (1:6, 7, 9). Now (10:25) Joshua passes on the encouragement he had received from Yahweh (cf. 2 Cor. 1:4).[10]

The Manner of Conquest (10:28-43)

Lastly, let us observe something of the manner of conquest. Our concern in this section is almost entirely with a historical issue.

In verses 28-39 the writer singles out six towns Joshua (and Israel) attacked and decimated in battle, while in verses 40-41 he summarises the geographical limits of the southern campaign.

The conquest here seems so decisive that some find problems when they arrive at Judges 1 where, apparently, so much of the conquest remains to be done by the individual tribes.

According to verse 43, after the southern campaign Joshua and Israel returned to camp at Gilgal, near the Jordan and what used to be Jericho. Such action implies that Joshua had no intention of occupying the (south) land at that point. Leaving the scene of her victories, Israel has little control over those sites (i.e. they could eventually be repopulated), although one could suppose that Israel had broken the backbone of Canaanite power in the region.

The phrase *pa'am 'ehat* in verse 42 lends support to this contention. This phrase is frequently translated 'at one time' (RSV, NASB) or 'in one campaign' (JB, NIV). However, Jeffrey Niehaus has made a careful study of the usage of *pa'am 'ehat* and related phrases and has concluded that the phrase, according to Old Testament idiom, must mean 'once' or 'one time' in Joshua 10:42. Hence the verse is not declaring that Joshua took the land all at one time, but that he took it once, which suggests 'the possibility that later battles were required to retake certain locales'.[11] In such a case, further tribal efforts are not surprising.

---

[10] I am indebted to Mr. John Toth, a former student, for this point.
[11] Jeffrey Niehaus, '*Pa'am 'Ehat* and the Israelite Conquest', *Vetus Testamentum* 30 (1980): 238. Cf. also what John Bright has said (*A History of Israel*, 3d ed. [Philadelphia: Westminster, 1981], 108) about Egyptian conquests in Canaan

The emphasis in Joshua 10 is on the fact that Joshua 'took' (Heb., *lakad*) the land or cities. To be sure, he 'smote' (*nakah*) populations and 'put them under the ban' (from the root *hrm*); but the overall emphasis is that Joshua took the cities and land (vv. 28, 32, 35, 37, 39, 42). This verb (*lakad*) must be carefully distinguished from various forms of *yarash* (to possess, dispossess, drive out), which dominates Judges 1 and denotes effective occupation of territory. Much of the problem of the conquest arises from a failure to distinguish the freight these two verbs carry. What has been 'lakaded' may need to be 're-lakaded' later; but what has been 'yarashed' has been definitely nailed down. Readers who desire more details may check the notes.[12]

The taking is no mean achievement; this too is Yahweh's gift (vv. 30, 32, 42).

STUDY QUESTIONS:

1. Why is the picture of Christ as a warrior so uncommon today?

---

during the Late Bronze Age: because 'conquest outran effective organisation' it had 'continually to be done over'. Is it unreasonable to assume that Israel faced the same necessity?

[12] I adapt the following from an earlier study ('A Proposed Life-Setting for the Book of Judges', University Microfilms [1978]: 94). The verb *yarash* (possess) is to be distinguished from *lakad* (take, capture) in the books of Joshua and Judges. They carry different connotations and are not to be confused. A study of the *relevant* data (i.e. where reference is to the taking of a city or territory and to the possession of territory or dispossession of populations; hence – for Hebrew buffs – the Qal of *lakad* fourteen times in Joshua alone, four times in Judges alone, two times in parallels; the Qal of *yarash* twelve times in Joshua, eight times in Judges; the Hiphil of *yarash* ten times in Joshua alone, eleven times in Judges alone, five times in parallels) in the two books will show that *lakad* involves initial conquest and *yarash* a continual effort or permanent settlement. A whole process is described in Dan's attack on Leshem (Laish) in Joshua 19:47: the tribe went up ('alah), fought (*laham*), took (*lakad*), smote (*nakah*), possessed (*yarash*), dwelt (*yashab*), and named (*qara'*) the place. Here the sequence suggests that *lakad* (between *laham* and *nakah*) is associated with initial onslaught and *yarash* (with *yashab* following) with permanent residence. Close attention to other texts in their contexts (e.g. Josh. 13:1; 18:1-3; 23:4-5) supports the same inference. Only Joshua 21:43 might appear to blur this distinction, but its character as a general summary statement explains its lack of precision. In light of all this, there is no need to question the traditional Hebrew text of Judges 1:18, nor is it then in conflict with verse 19, for they have reference to two different things. Nor is there any essential difficulty between Judges 1:8 and 1:21 when *lakad* and *yarash* are properly distinguished.

2. In what way does Christ as a warrior today?

3. Are you amazed when God answers your prayers? If so, why?

4. How do the sacraments (baptism and the Lord's Supper) encourage and strengthen your faith?

5. When you see victory in your life, do you often have to go back and get 're-victory?' What is the cause for the need of such 're-victory?'

10

Not by Chariots, Not by Horses
(Joshua 11:1-15)

Now the action takes place in the north of Palestine. Jabin king of Hazor is the ringleader of a coalition bent on stopping Israel. Hazor was apparently the dominating partner among these allies (cf. v. 10). Located at Tell el-Qedah, about ten miles north of the Sea of Chinnereth (Galilee), Hazor, in its Middle Bronze Age prime, was a massive site (the upper city was approximately 30 acres, the lower about 175 acres, with an estimated population of 40,000) that dominated the main branches of the Via Maris, the main highway leading from Egypt to Mesopotamia and Syria.[1] John J. Bimson has argued that it was this Middle Bronze (MB II C) Hazor that Joshua destroyed around 1430–1400 BC.[2]

Some of the other sites mentioned cannot be identified with certainty (e.g. Madon and Achshaph [v. 1]). But the references to the Arabah south of Chinnereth (the upper Jordan Valley [v. 2]), to the area of Dor near Mount Carmel on the Mediterranean (v. 2), to metropolitan Sidon (v. 8), and to Mount Hermon, located northeast of former Lake Huleh,

---

[1] Yigael Yadin, 'Hazor', *Archaeology*, Israel Pocket Library (Jerusalem: Keter Books, 1974), 92.

[2] John J. Bimson, *Redating the Exodus and Conquest*, Journal for the Study of the Old Testament/Supplement Series 5 (Sheffield, 1978), 185-200. In order to understand fully Bimson's argument one must read chapter 5 on 'Bichrome Ware and Ceramic Chronology' (pp. 147-83).

clearly place the main activity in the general area of Lower and Upper Galilee (see *The New Layman's Bible Commentary*, map 8, p. 322).

The Opponents of God's People (11:1-5)

Now let us press on into the text and observe how much space is given to depicting the opponents of God's people.

Think carefully about verses 1-5 for a moment and then come at them again. Have you ever wondered why the writer spills so much ink and wanders into such particular detail? Why he takes up so much of your time to specify various kings, to identify locations, to indicate ethnic groups opposing Israel? Why does he dwell on the massing of their numbers and their armaments? Why didn't the writer give you a break and make your Bible lighter and study brevity by saying, 'King Jabin summoned his confederates and their armies in order to make a massive assault on Israel'? But then the text would lose its punch. You see, it is precisely in reading this extended, detailed, particularising description of Israel's opposition that you begin to feel how overwhelming the enemy is, to sense in line-upon-line fashion the almost hopeless situation Israel faces. (More often than we know the Bible wants to impress our imaginations rather than merely inform our brains.)

There is a motive in this madness. To impress the reader (and Israel) with the massive resources available to the enemies of God makes the power of God shine more brightly in delivering his people from their hands. When we clearly see both Canaan's numerical (v. 4a) and technological (v. 4b) edge, we realise that Yahweh's strong right arm is no empty metaphor. 'When you go out to battle against your enemies and see horses and chariots plus an army larger than yours, you must not be afraid of them; for Yahweh your God is with you, the One who brought you up from the land of Egypt' (Deut. 20:1).

The Energy in God's Sovereignty (11:6-7)

Secondly, verses 6-7 contain an implicit recognition of the energy in God's sovereignty. Look at verses 6 and 7 side by side. In verse 6 Yahweh gives his sovereign assurance,

'I will hand all of them over to Israel, slain' (NIV); in verse 7 Joshua and Israel blast into the enemy camp in a surprise attack ('suddenly', hence probably at night?). I do not want to overplay the text. But isn't the sequence significant? Divine sovereignty does not negate human activity but stimulates it (see comments on 10:8-9). We frequently look at the teaching of divine sovereignty too simplistically. Some will allege that if God ordains something as certain it renders human effort irrelevant: 'Let's go and let God.' But Joshua knew better. His view was not to let go but to grab hold. Divine sovereignty creates confidence, which calls forth our effort even to the point of reckless abandon. God's sovereignty is not a doctrine that shackles us but a reality that liberates us, not a cloud that stifles but an elixir that invigorates.

Just a note here on Joshua's ingenuity and Jabin's geography will help us appreciate the event. Joshua attacked Jabin's forces in their camp 'by the waters of Merom' (v. 7). For our purposes it makes little difference whether Merom is located at Meirun or near Maroun er Ras, both of which are seven to eight miles from Hazor (southwest and northwest respectively).[3] The point is that Merom was in Upper Galilee, approximately 4,000 feet above sea level and not conducive to chariot manoeuvring.[4] Could it be that Merom was only an assembly point for Jabin's host and that they intended to encounter Joshua further south on the Plain of Esdraelon, where Canaanite 'tanks' could be used to real advantage?[5] In any case, Joshua's blitz negated any tactical advantage chariots or horses could give. Just because Yahweh promises victory (v. 6) is no reason not to use one's brains (v. 7).

---

[3] See Yohanan Aharoni, *The Land of the Bible: A Historical Geography*, rev. and enl. (Philadelphia: Westminster, 1979), 225-26. See the useful discussions of Gus W. Van Beek, 'Merom, Waters of', *IDB*, 3:356 (prefers Meirun/Meiron) and Anson F. Rainey, 'Merom, Waters of', *ZPED*, 4:192-93 (prefers Maroun er Ras).

[4] Marten H. Woudstra, *The Book of Joshua*, The New International Commentary on the Old Testament (Grand Rapids: Eerdmans , 1981), 191.

[5] John Gray (*Joshua, Judges and Ruth*, New Century Bible [Greenwood, S.C.: Attic, 1967], 119) alludes to an Egyptian text, which reveals that 'in rough country, such as the mountains of Galilee, the chariot was dismantled and reassembled in suitable terrain' (see James B. Pritchard, ed., *Ancient Near Eastern Texts Relating to the Old Testament*, 3d ed. [Princeton: Princeton University Press, 1969], 477). Hence my suggestion that Joshua may have hit while the matériel was in transit to more suitable chariot ground.

The Sufficiency of God's Help (11:6, 9)

The hamstringing of the enemy's horses and burning of their chariots emphasise the sufficiency of God's help (vv. 6, 9).

Hamstringing a horse made the animal militarily useless; it involved cutting the large tendon at the back of the knee on the hind legs. Some hold that the Israelites did this because they were untrained in the machinery of Canaanite hi-tech warfare and, not knowing how to use horses and chariots themselves, simply disabled and destroyed them.[6] However, the command probably stems more from divine vigilance than from human ignorance. Yahweh's intention is to teach Israel not to depend on such modes of assistance but to repose in God's help alone.[7] 'Some boast in chariots, some in horses, but *we*, we will boast in the name of Yahweh our God' (Ps. 20:7; see also Isa. 31:1-3). By prohibiting such means of normal human security, Yahweh instructs Israel to look only to the keeper of Israel (Ps. 121). This point does not conflict with that of verses 6-7 (human agency active under divine sovereignty). Divine help (vv. 6, 8) does not exclude human effort (v. 7) acting in faith on divine assurance, but it does forbid using human machinery as a substitute for God's aid (vv. 6b, 9). Sometimes, it becomes very difficult to discern the difference between the two. In any case, Yahweh insists that his people recognise that their help comes from Yahweh, maker of heaven and earth (Ps. 121:2); therefore he denies us some of our favourite props.

The Model of God's Servant (11:12, 15)

We can observe, fourthly, that Joshua seems to be presented as the model of God's servant. There is a hint of this in verse 12, but verse 15 is emphatic: 'As Yahweh had commanded Moses his servant, so Moses had commanded Joshua; and that is what Joshua did; he did not omit a thing of all that Yahweh commanded Moses.' The commands in question are those of Exodus 34:11-16, Numbers 33:51-54, and Deuteronomy 20:16-18 (cf. Num. 27:18-23; Deut. 3:21-22; 31:7-8, 23). Obedience meant

---

[6] H. W. Lay, 'Hamstring', *ISBE* (rev. ed.), 2:608; cf. Yehezkel Kaufmann, *The Religion of Israel* (New York: Schocken, 1960), 252-53.

[7] Cf. John Calvin, *Commentaries on the Book of Joshua*, trans. Henry Beveridge, in vol. 4 of *Calvin's Commentaries*, 22 vols. (reprint ed.; Grand Rapids: Baker, 1981), 169; Woudstra, *Joshua*, 191.

decimating and/or expelling the native population of Canaan (vv. 10-12, 14b of the present chapter). Naturally, we regard such commands as unnecessarily vicious, because we do not comprehend the contagious spiritual cancer that was throughout Canaan. We arrogantly pride ourselves on being kinder than God, but we only prove that we haven't a clue about what holiness is.

We may agree then with Trent C. Butler that the conquest narratives (chs. 2–11) stand

> as a monument to the great faithfulness of Joshua to the Mosiac law. It thus stands as a goal for all future leaders of Israel. Rather than being law makers, the kings of Israel are law takers and law keepers.[8]

That seems to be what verse 15 is saying: 'Here is a model of God's servant. His chief characteristic is that he obeys God's commands.' That sounds bland and nonthreatening enough, and commonplace. But it stands as a needed witness to Israel's future leaders and kings (and to individual Israelites) that what marks a model leader is not the size of his chariot force, the number of females in his harem, or the presence of peacocks in the royal zoo, but an obedience to God's commandments that leads God's people to be faithful. Surely we must admit that when we get wrapped up in all the glossy criteria of an evangelical success, 1 John 2:3 still cuts through all the flack. Even *the* servant of God had no other standard: 'I always do what pleases him' (John 8:29). Here is not only a high standard but also a liberating purge that can eliminate numerous secondary items from our cluttered agendas.

I want to include an additional note regarding the manner of the conquest, since verses 10-15 contain some important data about it.

The text clearly notes that Joshua burned Hazor (v. 11), but only Hazor, for verse 13 affirms that 'Israel did not burn all the cities standing on their mounds (tells)'. I take 'all the cities' to refer to those conquered in this northern campaign. Only Hazor was burned; the rest were not.

---

[8] Trent C. Butler, *Joshua*, Word Biblical Commentary (Waco: Word, 1983), 129.

We make several observations about the conquest in light of its execution in the north.

First, observe the relative silence of the biblical narratives in regard to the burning. Jericho (6:24), Ai (8:28), and Hazor (11:11) are specifically said to have been burned. I can think of no others. Our writer tells us that Israel burned none of the northern cities – except Hazor (11:11, 13). Might this not have been Israel's pattern in the conquest as a whole? Naturally, we must beware of arguing from silence; but it is not an unwarranted assumption when we have the pattern in the north clearly stated.

What does seem unwarranted is the way some reconstructions of the conquest based on archaeology seem to assume that Israel's practice must have been to burn conquered towns. Excavations show the burning and violent destruction of Bethel, Debir (if it is to be identified with Tell Beit Mirsim, which is doubtful), Lachish, Eglon (if it is Tell el-Hesi), and Hazor around 1250–1220 bc, and it has been common in some circles to attribute this destruction to Israel.[9] But on what grounds can one assume that because Israel burned three cities (according to the biblical text) they burned all or most? Especially when the biblical text does not say they burned, for example, Debir or Lachish? Especially when the text clearly declares they burned none in the north but Hazor? Moreover, even if, for the sake of argument, we supposed that Israel did burn most conquered towns, how could we be reasonably convinced that such late-thirteenth-century devastations could be attributed only to Israel? Such burning might have been the result of the influx of the Sea People, Egyptian attempts at control in Canaan, warfare among city-states, or local upheavals such as earthquake.[10] We can be certain that no burning resulted from a short in a Canaanite microwave – but of other possible causes it is difficult to establish that Israel was the instigator, since no one left calling cards.[11]

---

[9] See John Bright, *A History of Israel*, 3d ed. (Philadelphia: Westminster, 1981), 130-32, for a brief recap of this data.

[10] See Bimson, *Redating the Exodus and Conquest*, 53-56.

[11] In this argument I am not casting doubt on the historicity of the conquest but on

Second, observe how foolish it would have been for Israel to make a practice of burning towns. Couldn't Israel, if they were going eventually to settle the land, use cities and houses? Their practice in the Transjordan conquest reveals this (Num. 21:25), their Torah expects this (Deut. 6:10-12; 19:1), their restraint in the north assumes this (Josh. 11:11, 13), and their leader declares this (Josh. 24:13). Hence I would not expect to find much evidence for the conquest in terms of wholesale destruction of material culture. The biblical witness firmly supports this position. Granted, Israel was to rip down all Baal chapels and 'Our Lady Asherah' shrines (Exod. 34:13-16), but that did not mean they couldn't sleep in a Canaanite house or hold court in a Canaanite city gate.

STUDY QUESTIONS:

1. In what ways do you see 'Yahweh's strong right arm' at work against his enemies in today's culture?

2. Does Yahweh's sovereignty make you 'let go' or 'grab hold?'

3. Do you think the phrase, "put feet to your prayers" takes away from the sufficiency of God's help or is it a recognition of your responsibility within God's sovereignty?

4. Why was it important to show Joshua as a leader who obeyed the commandments of God?

5. If Joshua did not burn all of the cities, why then were these three the only ones burned? Why not burn all of the cities they conquered?

the accuracy of one reconstruction of it. The argument does not dispute the biblical picture but undercuts one of the main props for the late date (thirteenth-century) view of the conquest.

11

War Wrap-up
(Joshua 11:16-23)

This section is a self-contained unit (note how it opens and closes with 'so Joshua took all the/this land', vv. 16, 23), which broadly recaps the extent of the whole conquest. References in verses 16-17 to 'hill country', the Negeb (south country), Mount Halak (probably southwest of the Dead Sea), and Mount Hermon (far to the north) show that our summary includes more than the northern campaign of 11:1-15. Let us isolate the key concerns of this section.

The Demands of Yahweh's Call (11:18)
First of all, verse 18 shows us how demanding Yahweh's call is: 'Joshua carried on war a long time (lit. many days) with all these kings.' George Bush is certainly correct:

> It would seem that the writer by inserting this statement here designed to guard the reader against the impression that, as the record of these wars is very brief, so the space of time in which they were accomplished was also brief.[1]

We seldom realise how highly condensed the Bible is. (It has to be in order to remain portable!) So the unsuspecting reader

---

[1] George Bush, *Notes, Critical and Practical, on the Book of Joshua* (Chicago: Henry A. Sumner, 1881), 136.

may get a false impression, namely, that just because it takes less than twenty minutes to read Joshua 10–11 (which, for the most part, are condensed reports), it must not have taken long for those events to have transpired. Hence verse 18 serves as a mental corrector; 'Joshua carried on war a long time.'

The conquest then was a long, gruelling, demanding process. Joshua 2–11 rightly gives you the highlights; but you must not think it was merely one hot summer's work.[2] Israel knew this. Yahweh had told them, 'I will not drive them out from before you in one year, lest the land become desolate and the wild beasts multiply against you. Little by little I will drive them out...' (Exod. 23:29-30, rsv; cf. Deut. 7:22). To be sure, God's power was at work but in such a way as to call for endurance and tenacity from his people.

I do not want to get caught in soupy spiritualisation here. However, it may be proper to point out that this remains one of God's patterns with his people. God's power still works among us (cf. Phil. 2:13), not necessarily in quick flashes but over a long time, which calls for simple, durable fidelity over such time. Even though God is at work, many days still consist of washing your face, brushing your teeth, taking out garbage, and attending class. That is why 'you have need of *endurance*' (Heb. 10:36).

The Fearfulness of Yahweh's Hardening (11:19-20)

Secondly, verses 19-20 stress how fearful Yahweh's hardening is. The Gibeonites were the only ones who concluded peace with Israel; all the others encountered Israel in battle, and they did so because Yahweh hardened their hearts. The writer does not hold Gibeon up as a model of the proper response; he merely notes her as an exception to the universal response.[3] The burden of the text is to explain why Canaan's cities were gripped by this passion to meet Israel in battle,

---

[2] For the calculation that it may have taken five to seven years, see the commentaries.

[3] We are not to construe verse 19a as suggesting that Canaan's cities were expected to make peace with Israel or even were initially offered peace by Israel. The verse is not implying a principle but only noting an exception. Theoretically, one might argue that if a city had sought peace and had converted to Yahwism, Yahweh might well have instructed Joshua to spare it (see Matthew Henry, *Commentary on the Whole Bible*, 6 vols. [New York: Revell, n.d.], 2:52).

to disclose how it was that they willingly walked into their own destruction. The theology of the text clarifies the matter: Yahweh hardened their hearts that they might be utterly destroyed, that they might make no plea for grace,[4] that they might be exterminated.

We have in verse 20 what is sometimes called judicial hardening. The Canaanite's day of grace has passed (Gen. 15:16); their iniquity is now full; there has been no turning away from but persistence in their idolatrous and sex-perverting worship; and so Yahweh 'gives them up', confirms them in that resistance, and leads them by it to destruction (compare Pharaoh in Exodus 4–14, and Paul's repeated 'God gave them up' in Romans 1:24, 26, 28).

But let us react to the sheer audacity of this text: 'for it was Yahweh's doing to harden their hearts ... in order to utterly destroy them'. Do we not find that disturbing, offensive, outrageous? Who gave God the right to be that sovereign? But our verdict had better remain stuck in our throat. Don't try to evade the clarity of this text. It is a fearful thing to fall into the hands of the living God. Don't think you can escape this God by running into the New Testament; you will meet the same God there (Heb. 3:12-13). You will do better to tremble – and worship.

The Needlessness of Our Fears (11:21-22)
We see, lastly, how needless our fears are. Of course, the very mention of the Anakim probably doesn't send chills up your spine, because you've never seen any of them. Who were they? They were the incredible hulks of the land of Canaan (Num. 13:28, 31-33; Deut. 1:26-28; 9:1-2). Forty years before, Israel was sure that even God's help was of no avail against these big bruisers. In Israel's dictionary Anakim spelled terror.

That is why it is so interesting to meet the Anakim here in Joshua 11 and to read that Joshua 'cut (them) off'.[5] Remember

---

[4] The RSV translates 'should receive no mercy'; but the predominant meaning of *tehinnah* in the Old Testament is 'plea for grace' or 'supplication for grace', rather than simply 'grace' or 'mercy'.

[5] See Marten H. Woudstra, *The Book of Joshua*, The New International Commentary on the Old Testament (Grand Rapids: Eerdmans, 1981), 197-98, on the relation of 11:21-22 to 15:13-19.

that verses 16-23 are an overall summary of the whole conquest. Hence it is fascinating to see that the last entry in this overview of the conquest is the defeat of the Anakim. Here God exposes the groundlessness of the fear and unbelief of the Numbers 13 generation. Our most dreadful fears are subject to Yahweh's power.

I do not want to trivialise this text by chatting about the giants in your life. But neither do I want to leave this text unapplied. Surely this text at least means to assure us that Yahweh's power is adequate to meet our most dreadful fears. Our situation is both different from and similar to Israel's. The form of our fears is different; the adequacy of our God is the same.

In *Pilgrim's Progress* John Bunyan describes Christian's approach to the Palace Beautiful where he hoped to get lodging. He began to walk down a very narrow passage leading to the porter's lodge. Then he saw two lions in the way. Bunyan adds parenthetically: 'The lions were chained; but he saw not the chains.' That is frequently our case – we fear because we don't see the chains. Yet the fact that Christ sits at the Father's right hand 'far above all rule and authority and power and dominion' and has 'all things under his feet' (Eph. 1:20-22) means that every power that would destroy us is chained. But, sometimes, we don't see the chains.

STUDY QUESTIONS:

1. Are you patient or impatient when it comes to seeing God's working in your life or circumstances?

2. What is meant by God 'hardening their hearts?' Why is this difficult to understand?

3. Are there still those today whose hearts God hardens which makes no plea for grace?

4. What fears might you have that constantly challenge your trust in God?

5. Why does fear get in the way of your trust in God? Why does it not allow you to move forward?

12

Great Is Thy Faithfulness
(Joshua 12)

You might think I could do readers a kindness by foregoing comment on chapter 12. It appears to be sheer tedium. After all, 'the king of Hormah, one; the king of Arad, one; the king of Libnah, one; the king of Adullam, one' (vv. 14-15) does not exactly engulf the reader in a glow of devotional warmth. How can pondering such material prepare you for a day at the office or on the tractor?

Let us begin with verses 1-6. Why resurrect the shades of these two kings who used to rule the east of the Jordan? Sihon's domain covered roughly the southern half of Transjordan and big Og's (cf. Deut. 3:11) was the northern half. The story of their defeat appears in Numbers 21:21-35; Moses' commentary on it comes at Deuteronomy 2:26–3:11. Just as Pontius Pilate has earned a permanent niche in the Apostles' Creed, so Sihon and Og appear in Israel's praises and prayers (Pss. 135:11; 136:19-20; Neh. 9:22; cf. Deut. 31:4). But why dig them up here? Why not let sleeping kings lie?

Guard the Unity of Yahweh's People (12:1-6)

One answer to this question is that the writer wants to guard the unity of Yahweh's people.[1] (See notes on 1:12-18.) The two-

---

[1] Marten H. Woudstra, The Book of Joshua, The New International Commentary on the Old Testament (Grand Rapids: Eerdmans, 1981), 200.

and-a-half eastern tribes feared the day might come when they would be regarded as non-Israel by the western tribes (22:21-29), that the majority settled in Canaan proper would exclude them from the circle of Yahweh's people. So the writer of Joshua carefully includes in the survey of conquered kings the record of the conquest of Sihon and Og; as if to say, 'Remember Yahweh gave victories east of the Jordan too; don't forget Israel lives over there as well.'

Nor can the church deny that she needs to hear this word. Of course, there is always the classic difficulty of those who confess the same Lord relegating their brothers to Christ's subflock (at best). So Arminians might do to Calvinists and Calvinists to charismatics, and so on. But this can happen even within a local fellowship of God's people. Some believers seem to feel (and give the impression) that others in the fellowship don't quite belong. Perhaps because of economic circumstances (cf. James 2:1-9); or because they are different in personality or taste; maybe they do not exude that bubbly, energetic, upbeat, middle-class, victorious-life air; they have been involved in a divorce or separation; or they are not as biblically or doctrinally knowledgable as the 'in' group. Strange how we forget that all whom God chose were losers. This is why the apostle told the cocky Corinthians simply to look at themselves and they would see that 'God chose what is foolish in the world ... God chose what is weak in the world ... God chose what is low and despised in the world' (1 Cor. 1:27-28). Strange how old Sihon and Og, being dead, yet speak!

Vindicate the Fidelity of Yahweh's Promise (12:7-24)
Secondly, this chapter means to vindicate the fidelity of Yahweh's promise. Such is the function of verses 7-24, the bulk of which is a listing of thirty-one conquered kings. The list only appears monotonous; John Calvin assessed it correctly:

> But though each of those now summarily mentioned was previously given more in detail, there is very good reason for here placing before our eyes as it were a living picture of the goodness of God, proving that there had been a complete ratification and performance of the covenant made with Abraham as given in the

words, 'Unto thy seed will I give this land.' (Gen. xii.7; xiii.15; xx.18.)[2]

Joshua 12:7-24 emphasises that Yahweh's old promise to Abraham in Genesis 15:18-21 has been fulfilled. 'God was able to do what he had promised' (Rom. 4:21). These verses do not drip with tedium; they tingle with excitement. 'The king of Tappuah, one; the king of Hepher, one' (v. 17) – those words are not an excerpt from a dull archive; they are the lyrics of a song! Verses 7-24 constitute the stanzas for Israel's version of 'Great Is Thy Faithfulness'. Yahweh's ancient word has proven faithful.

Provide an Itemisation of Yahweh's Goodness
Another point is related to our second observation. The detailed listing of conquered kings provides an itemisation of Yahweh's goodness (see the quote from Calvin). As we have said, this is not tedium but thanksgiving, not just in general but in particular and in detail. Each conquered king is specified; each is a sign of Yahweh's power and a cause for Israel's praise. H. L. Ellison has put it well:

> It would be unfair to suggest that the Church is unwilling to thank God for all His many mercies, but on the whole it is unwilling to indulge in detailed and specific thanks. If we were to train ourselves to recognize God's goodness act by act and detail by detail, many of us would come to think more highly both of God and of the Church. Much of our despondency comes from failing to see how much God has really achieved.[3]

Itemising Yahweh's goodness – that is always the method of biblical faith (see Pss. 105, 135, 136). It is as faith gives thanks in detail that faith is nurtured, encouraged, and takes on fresh heart to expect more mercies. Hence we should get rid of some of the tripe in our prayers like 'and thank you for your many,

---

[2] John Calvin, *Commentaries on the Book of Joshua*, trans. Henry Beveridge, in vol. 4 of *Calvin's Commentaries*, 22 vols. (reprint ed.; Grand Rapids: Baker, 1981), 178.

[3] H. L. Ellison, *Scripture Union Bible Study Books: Joshua – 2 Samuel* (Grand Rapids: Eerdmans, 1966), 13.

many blessings'. Name one or two of those blessings instead. Why do we use such general 'lingo-ese' in our prayers (and, worse yet, teach it to our children)?

Foreshadow the Coming of Yahweh's Victory
Since chapter 12 serves as a summary of the conquest to date, we can rightly hold that as such it foreshadows the coming of Yahweh's victory.[4] The victory of Yahweh achieved over Sihon, Og, and Canaan's kings is both a preview and a pledge of that time when 'the kingdom of the world (will) become the kingdom of our Lord and of his Christ, and he shall reign for ever and ever' (Rev. 11:15). Every one of Yahweh's victories over his enemies in the process of history is a partial portrayal of his victory over all his enemies at the consummation of history.[5] This is meant to steel and strengthen his suffering people as they long for that grand finale.

STUDY QUESTIONS:

1. How might the church be guilty of not showing unity within the body-life of the church?

2. So far God has shown himself to be a faithful God. Why does Israel need such continued assurance?

3. How does God assure you of his faithfulness?

4. The hymn states, "Count your blessings, name them one by one…" does such itemizing of your blessings indicate a trusting faith in God?

5. Does seeing the victories in the Old Testament give you hope for the final victory in Christ?

---

[4] Woudstra, *Joshua*, 200; Karl Gutbrod, *Das Buch vom Lande Gottes*, Die Botschaft des Alten Testaments, 3d ed. (Stuttgart: Calwer, 1965), 101.
[5] Note how Judges 5:31 in light of its preceding context supports this contention.

Part 3

Possessing the Land

(Joshua 13–21)

13

Receiving Our Inheritance
(Joshua 13)

With chapter 13 we enter another major division of the Book of Joshua; this division extends through chapter 21. So far we have:

Entering the land, chapters 1–4
Taking the land, chapters 5–12
Possessing the land, chapters 13–21

Probably even the most stout-hearted reader of Joshua begins to crumble and nod as he enters chapters 13–21. Watching war movies always tends to be more exciting than participating in land surveys. Insomnia naturally thrives on accounts of dry riverbeds or crumbling walls. Somehow chasing a Canaanite out of the hill country is far more stimulating than plodding over his former land counting villages and tracing borders.

Our problem is that we are too detached. Insofar as possible we must see this land distribution as an Israelite would have seen it.

In my study I use an old wooden study chair. The seating material long ago disintegrated and was replaced by a solid piece of masonite screwed into the frame of the seat. A chunk of old board has been added beneath the seat for support. Some additional wire has been installed where necessary.

One could pick up a splinter without much effort. Now if my study were your study, probably one of your first acts would be to rid yourself of that old study chair and get a 'decent' one. Why? Because that chair means nothing to you. Why do I use it? Because it means something to me. It was my father's chair, repaired in his own way, and he gave it to me. Hence it interests me and I prize it, because it is – you might say – part of my inheritance. If you could look at it as I do, you might view it differently. Now that is what we must force ourselves to do with Joshua 13–21. You might think these lists and descriptions terribly dull, but for the Israelite this material describes his inheritance. What's dull about that? Yahweh had promised 'to your seed I will give this land' (Gen. 12:7), and now Abraham's grandchildren (generations removed) could walk into wadis and count towns that form the particulars of that promise.

In chapter 13 we find two main sections, verses 1-7, which introduce all of chapters 13–21, and verse 8-33, which detail the territory that the two-and-a-half Transjordan tribes had already been allotted by Moses. However, our exposition will ignore this structural difference and treat the chapter as a whole.

A Sufficient Promise (13:1-7)

Observe, first, how Israel receives a sufficient promise (vv. 1-7, especially v. 6b). Joshua had now become old; there was yet much land to occupy; Yahweh's power was adequate for the task ahead; Joshua had only to allot to the tribes their particular inheritances for them to clean out and occupy.

It is easy to read verse 1 ('very much of the land remains to be possessed', NASB) and to forget just how much had been accomplished under Joshua's leadership. A careful look at 'the land that remains' shows that it consists of the Philistine corridor (vv. 2-4a) in the southwest of Canaan and, in the north, a swath of territory about fifty miles wide (vv. 4-6a), the northern edge of which extended inward to Lebo-Hamath, almost fifty miles north of Damascus![1] All this land was, in

---

[1] See Yohanan Aharoni, *The Land of the Bible: A Historical Geography*, rev. and enl. (Philadelphia: Westminster, 1979), 233-39, and Yohanan Aharoni and Michael Avi-Yonah, *The Macmillan Bible Atlas,* rev. ed. (New York: Macmillan, 1977), 50-51.

one sense, on the edges of Israel's land. If such was the land that remained, it implies that Israel had achieved a significant measure of dominance in the main part of Canaan. Not that such dominance was total, but it was substantial. Joshua and Israel's conquests apparently caused a power vacuum into which Israel could step. Now it was time to allot the land to tribes who would follow up and extend the conquest (vv. 6b-7).

Nor were the tribes left merely to their own stamina but stood under the assurance of Yahweh's promise: 'I [emphatic] will drive them out from before the sons of Israel' (v. 6b).

That promise looks a bit wild in light of the map, since it prods Israel to aim for dominance far north of Sidon and as far as Lebo-Hamath.[2] But then Yahweh's promises frequently are wild, as Abraham and a few others could attest. God's promises take in the scope of his will for us, not merely the limits of what we think to be likely. Nor must we miss the setting of this promise. In chapter 1 Yahweh's promise came in the face of Moses' death, here in the face of Joshua's age. Joshua is not dead, but he is of such age that he will no longer be 'going out and coming in' before Israel's army. Joshua is about to retire but Yahweh will continue to be adequate. 'You have become old ... I will drive them out' (vv. 1, 6). The mortality of his servants never handicaps the everlasting God.

A Dangerous Sign (13:8-13)

Secondly, we should note a dangerous sign of Israel's waning vigilance (v. 13). In verses 8-13 we have a general description of the boundaries of the land possessed by the tribes that settled east of the Jordan, which closes with the exception of verse 13: 'But the sons of Israel did not dispossess (or, drive out) the Geshurites and the Maacathites; so Geshur and Maacath reside in the midst of Israel to this day.' (Geshur was northeast of the Sea of Galilee and Maacath was north of Geshur.) We will hear more such statements later (Josh. 15–17; Judg. 1), but this is the first of a series of what I regard as accusations of

---

[2] The northern boundary sketched in Numbers 34 and Joshua 13 was that of the Egyptian district of Canaan during the fourteenth and thirteenth centuries BC; see Aharoni, *Land of the Bible*, 74-75, and *Macmillan Bible Atlas*, 41.

tribal failure to follow up the initial conquest. It was one thing to invade and conquer a territory; it was another to persevere over a period of time to occupy the whole territory allotted to a tribe. Verse 13 seems matter-of-fact enough; incomplete obedience usually is. It brings no immediate crisis. It seldom does. However, here is testimony to all God's people: we frequently and strangely prove faithful in the great crisis of faith, remain steadfast in severe storms, perhaps even relish the excitement of the heaviest assaults, yet lack the tenacity, the dogged endurance, the patient plodding often required in the prosaic affairs of believing life; we are often loath to be faithful in (what we regard as) little.

Repeated Encouragement (13:8-33)
Further, we cannot help detecting a note of repeated encouragement throughout verses 8-33. As stated, verses 8-13 contain a general description of the boundaries of the Transjordan possession; the rest outlines in more detail the inheritance of Reuben (vv. 15-23), Gad (vv. 24-28), and half of Manasseh (vv. 29-31). Roughly, Reuben's inheritance (the southernmost) stretched from the Arnon River north to Heshbon, Gad's from Heshbon up to Mahanaim (near or on the Jabbok River) with a sliver of land reaching up to the Sea of Galilee (Chinnereth), and half-Manasseh's from Mahanaim up to and including all of Bashan. All this seems like so many lakes, rivers, valleys, plains, and towns all jumbled together. However, we must not miss the repeated allusions to Israel's victories over our old friends Sihon and Og (vv. 10, 12, 21, 27, 30-31), not to mention Balaam (v. 22; see Num. 22–25; 31:8). What does this mean? It means that throughout all this geography and topography there are constant allusions to the victories Yahweh had previously given Israel under Moses. The allusions jog Israel's memory and fortify their faith in face of any contemporary enemies; for it is in remembering how Yahweh handled Sihon and Og (Pss. 135:10-12; 136:17-22) that Israel finds assurance that Yahweh will still have compassion on his servants and that his covenant love persists into present prime time as well (Pss. 135:14; 136:19b, 20b). This is the biblical prescription for faith; faith finds both steadfastness

and expectancy by rehearsing and revelling in Yahweh's past acts of faithfulness.

The True Inheritance

Lastly, in this section the writer points the people of God to their true inheritance. He does this in the two notes about the Levites. They were exceptional in that they did not receive a land allotment like the other tribes. Rather, Levi's inheritance consisted of the offerings by fire (or 'food offerings' or 'gifts'?)[3] belonging to Yahweh (v. 14) or, quite plainly, of Yahweh himself (v. 33). However, any believing Israelite could come to adopt this Levite perspective, realising that, above all else, Yahweh himself was his 'portion in the land of the living' (Ps. 142:5), indeed his 'portion forever' (Ps. 73:26).[4] This does not mean that a truly spiritual Israelite would regard his land inheritance as so much dirt. No, faith always prizes the land as Yahweh's gift (Ps. 37:3, 9, 11, 22, 29, 34). But healthy, grateful faith sees beyond the inheritance to the one who granted it and is careful never to prize Yahweh's gifts more than Yahweh himself. Hence Levi – and Israel – should say, 'Yahweh is my inheritance, my portion.' He remains such, even if the land be taken away (Lam. 3:24 in context).

Study Questions:

1. What possible 'limits' might you claim that you believe would limit God's power? (For example, old age, poor location, etc…)

2. What happens when you allow the 'little things' in your life to remain unchecked? How might it hurt you in the long run?

3. Why is it when the crisis is past that we let down our defenses against sin and Satan?

---

[3] On the term *'ishsheh* (traditionally 'offerings by fire'), cf. Gordon J. Wenham, *The Book of Leviticus*, The New International Commentary on the Old Testament (Grand Rapids: Eerdmans, 1979), 56, and P. C. Craigie, *The Book of Deuteronomy*, The New International Commentary on the Old Testament (Grand Rapids: Eerdmans, 1976), 258-59.

[4] 'Portion' renders the Hebrew *ḥeleq*, a term closely related to 'inheritance' (*naḥalah*).

4. Why is the recounting of God's past acts of faithfulness so important? What does this do for Israel? For you?

5. As a believer you have received an inheritance. Do you view the gift of salvation more than the Giver of salvation?

14

For Example
(Joshua 14)

How often we run into that little Latin abbreviation *e.g.* (*exempli gratia*), 'for example'. Joshua 14 seems to be primarily an e.g. This chapter points to Caleb as an example of how Israel's tribes ought to be extending the original conquest by cleaning out and nailing down their various tribal portions.

Chapter 14 opens a section dealing with the tribal allotments in the land of Canaan (i.e. the land west of the Jordan River). It opens up a section of material that ends at 19:51 (cf. 14:1). This section opens and closes with the two faithful spies (see Num. 13–14) receiving their respective inheritances, Caleb in 14:6-15 and Joshua in 19:49-50.[1] But chapters 14–17 also form a given block of material, for Caleb's adventuresome faith in 14:6-15 deliberately contrasts with the hesitant caution of the Joseph tribes in 17:14-18. More on this later, however.

Before attacking the Caleb section we should give attention to the introduction in verses 1-5. While verses 3-4 explain why only nine and a half tribes received portions in Canaan (two and a half tribes received theirs east of the Jordan, minus Levi who would not receive an allotment as such but only

---

[1] Marten H. Woudstra, *The Book of Joshua*, the New International Commentary on the Old Testament (Grand Rapids: Eerdmans, 1981), 296.

cities to live in, plus Joseph, which actually constituted two tribes, Ephraim and Manasseh, equals, all in all, twelve tribes; two and a half east of Jordan, nine and a half west of Jordan), verses 2 and 5 underscore that they carried out the procedure 'as Yahweh had commanded Moses' (see Num. 26:55). Such a matter probably doesn't interest us much – it's only a note about obedience. But perhaps it suggests a useful correction – that obedience in the more prosaic duties is as important to Yahweh as in the more explosive, dynamic events. No command of Yahweh is ever trivial, and, therefore, all obedience is both necessary and significant.

The Devotion of Faith (14:7-8)
Now let us look at verses 6-15 where the writer displays Caleb's ideal response of faith. First of all, we see the devotion of faith. Caleb remembers the episodes of Numbers 13–14, when Moses sent twelve spies from Kadesh-barnea to investigate the land of Canaan. The majority report of the spies 'caused the people's heart to melt' (v. 8) – Canaan's cities were highly fortified and their military were such big bruisers; why, Israel would be like a junior-high football team playing the Dallas Cowboys (Num. 13:31-33). Caleb, however, had the gall to go against the flow: 'But I [emphatic in Hebrew] completely followed Yahweh my God' (a fact noted three times in this passage [vv. 8, 9, 14]). That is the devotion of faith. And it meant that Caleb (along with Joshua) had the courage to stand alone and give a minority report (Num. 13:30) even though it nearly cost him his life (Num. 14:6-10). We can possess the land; Yahweh is with us; stop fearing those big phantoms. Such was Caleb's report.

Hence the devotion of faith required courage, a willingness to stand alone, to go against the grain. The devotion of faith led to the isolation of faith. Such is often the case. The Christian teenager knows what this is like, when he or she must go against the moral-ethical flow of high-school culture. The Christian executive who tells his superior that he must either resign or be transferred to another department, because he refuses to line up prostitutes for the company's weekend visitors – that man knows this loneliness. Even pastors know a good bit of this. So you will not baptise the grandchild of a church member because the parents are not believers? Or you have the gall, along with the other elders, to place someone under church discipline? You may seek to follow the Lord completely and at the same time reduce church membership. God's people then must be prepared, for devoted faith frequently means lonely faith. And yet when Paul alluded to his first defence and lamented that 'everyone deserted me', he added in the next breath, 'But the Lord stood at my side and gave me strength' (2 Tim. 4:16-17, NIV).

But let me yank you back into BC again. This account of Caleb's lonely faith may have preached powerfully to Israel shortly after they settled in Canaan (cf. Judg. 2:6-23). As more and more Israelites began to settle into the rhythm of Canaanite nature worship and bend the knee to Baal, somehow preferring the orgasms of Baal to the commands of Yahweh, the remnant devoted to Yahweh would likely feel the pull to conform, to compromise, to walk the path of syncretism. They were hardly on the cutting edge of recent religious faith and life. They did not enjoy standing alone. But they could remember Caleb, who hadn't flinched to follow Yahweh completely even though it isolated him from human favour. It is not difficult to see how this Caleb tradition would frequently bolster the faith of God's beleaguered remnant at many points in Israel's history.

The Anchor of Faith

Throughout the passage Caleb refers to the anchor of faith. When Caleb approaches Joshua, he bases his request on 'the word that Yahweh spoke to Moses' (v. 6) about him. He keeps coming back to this: 'as he [Yahweh] promised' (v. 10a); 'from the time Yahweh spoke this word to Moses' (v. 10b); 'which Yahweh promised on that day' (v. 12a); 'as Yahweh has promised' (v. 12b). See also verse 9a, 'so Moses swore on that day....' Five times Caleb hammers this point home; his request is for nothing but what God had promised him (v. 9). True faith always functions that way; it pleads God's promises; it anchors itself upon the word of God. There can be no other foundation for faith.

Once I had a group of young people and adults in a new members' class. I held up a dollar bill (I was afraid to wager more for fear they did have faith) and spoke particularly to specific young people. I said: 'I will give this dollar bill to you.' Then I asked them how they would show they had faith in my word. As I recall, there were various responses. Some wondered if I would really part with a bona fide buck. Others replied that one would show faith by coming up and taking the dollar. Naturally, when they said that I had to turn to offer it to someone else. Finally, one lad didn't talk at all – he just walked up and grabbed the dollar. That was faith – acting on my word.

That is Caleb's faith and biblical faith – acting upon the word of God. We can easily make mistakes here. We try to base our faith on our feelings. If so, we will feel like unbelievers a good deal of the time! Sometimes we place our faith in faith; that is, we believe that if we have enough faith we will be able to weather the storm (which means that, somehow, we must pump up the faith). We forget that great faith is not so necessary as genuine faith (Luke 17:5-6). The object of faith, by definition, is God (not faith). 'It is not so much great faith in God that is required as faith in a great God.'[2] Caleb's is the biblical pattern. If we are Caleb's disciples we will take the promises of God, turn them into prayers, and plead them back to God.[3] (Certainly, we need to take care that we properly interpret the promises.) 'I wait for the Lord, my soul waits, and in his word I hope' (Ps. 130:5). I must not trust how spiritual I feel but what has gone forth from God's sacred mouth.

The Perspective of Faith (14:10-11)
In verses 10-11 Caleb reveals the perspective of faith: 'And now, look how Yahweh has kept me alive, as he promised, these forty-five years ... and now look how I am today eighty-five years old, yet I remain as strong today as the day when Moses sent me off; my strength is the same now as then for war and for going out and coming in.' This is the way of biblical faith – it remembers what Yahweh has done, and remembers

---

[2] Leon Morris, *The Gospel According to St. Luke*, Tyndale New Testament Commentaries (Grand Rapids: Eerdmans, 1974), 256.
[3] I believe this turn of expression comes from Alec Motyer, but I do not recall from which of his works.

in gratitude. So Caleb, as he builds to his punchline in verse 12, remembers Yahweh's goodness to date. Yahweh had kept him alive through the last forty-five years (cf. Ps. 33:18-19). This was no small bounty, since it was through war and wilderness. And Yahweh was still blessing him with strength and stamina, old as he was. This is the way faith looks at things; faith is always looking into the past, seeing God's goodness there, dragging it into the present, pondering it, praising for it, and so going on from strength to strength. The perspective of faith takes in God's goodness, responds in gratitude, and finds grace for God's next call.

The Energy of Faith (14:12)
Fourthly, Caleb displays the energy of faith. He now gets to his specific request: 'And now,[4] give me this hill country which Yahweh promised on that day, for *you* heard on that day how the Anakim were there and how there were large, fortified cities; perhaps Yahweh will be with me and I shall drive them out (or, dispossess) as Yahweh promised' (v. 12). So Joshua gave Caleb Hebron as his inheritance.

What accounts for such vigour and expectancy in this senior citizen of Israel? His vivid recollection of Yahweh's goodness and mercy in the past (vv. 10-11) certainly helps to explain his current boldness. But verse 12 itself suggests two facts that shot the adrenalin into Caleb's faith. One was the extreme difficulty of the task. It is as if Caleb says to Joshua: 'You remember the sneers you and I heard that day when the other ten spies brought the majority report? Remember all that whimpering about large, fortified cities and large, swaggering Anakim? And how all they could say for days was, "We are not able"? Well, that's exactly why I want this inheritance – there are fortified cities and real, live Anakim.' Precisely what caused Israel to shrink from this task in Numbers 13 gave Caleb the passion to assume it.

I remember reading a story Kennedy Smartt related in the *Presbyterian Journal* a few years ago. An American shoe company sent a salesman to a foreign country. He had hardly

---

[4] This is the third and climactic 'and now' in Caleb's speech; the two previous occurrences were in verse 10.

arrived before he cabled for money to come home. His reason: 'No one over here wears shoes.' The company brought him back and sent another salesman over. Soon he cabled: 'Send me all the shoes you can manufacture. The market is absolutely unlimited. No one here has shoes.'

So the sheer difficulty of the task stimulated Caleb's request. But we must remember – if we believe Numbers 13 – this is not because Caleb was an optimist whereas the Israelites had been realists, but because Caleb was a believer whereas the Israelites had refused to be.

Another factor fanned Caleb's faith: the unguessable favour of the Lord. 'Perhaps Yahweh will be with me and I shall dispossess them as Yahweh has promised' (v. 12b). Caleb's 'perhaps' is not the voice of doubt but of expectancy. ('As Yahweh has promised' shows that the outcome is certain. I suppose one could argue that Caleb could not be sure that he would be Yahweh's instrument in driving out the enemy, but such items are really beside the point.) Caleb's 'perhaps', however, both preserves and recognises the freedom of God. Caleb does not view Yahweh as his errand boy who must follow his orders but as the free and sovereign Lord who does whatever he pleases (Ps. 135:6). But because of Yahweh's promise (see, e.g. Exod. 23:29-30) Caleb suspects that Yahweh will be pleased to drive out the enemy before him. He is confident but not cocky. Biblical faith will always keep this tension; it will not dictate to the sovereign God or write his script for him – 'perhaps Yahweh will'; yet it will not doubt God when it can cling to any clear promise in the matter – 'as Yahweh has promised'. Taken as a whole Caleb's words in verse 12 simply exude expectancy. 'Perhaps ... it may be ... who knows ... what Yahweh will be pleased to do if I throw myself into this situation!' There is, I suppose, such a thing as mathematical faith that refuses to move unless it has worked it all out on its calculator. And then there is this faith that looks upon a faithful, almighty God, who delights to surprise his people with his goodness, a faith that loves to venture itself on such a God.

The Model of Faith

Though chapter 17 is a few chapters away, we must touch on it here, because it relates to 14:6-15, where Caleb is the model of faith.

Let us retrace the ground a bit. Chapters 14–17 depict in some detail the land west of the Jordan inherited by Judah (14:6–15:63) and the Joseph tribes (16:1–17:18). Here is a large block of material (14:6–17:18) that the writer has enclosed within a highly significant introduction (14:6-15) and tail piece (17:14-18). The former relates the confidence of Caleb, the latter the complaint of the Josephites in relation to pinning down the land. The pieces, I think, are direct and deliberate contrasts: the initiative of faith (14:6-15) is pitted against the hesitancy of fear (17:14-18).[5]

In Caleb's speech (14:6-12) we hear repeated reference to what Yahweh or Moses has promised (vv. 6, 9, 10 [twice], 12 [twice]), remember how Caleb completely followed Yahweh even when it was unpopular (vv. 8, 9, 14), and feel the energy that relishes facing formidable obstacles simply because he anticipates Yahweh's help (vv. 11-12).

What a contrast this forms to the complaints of the Joseph tribes (17:14-18)! Here is a numerous people (v. 14) but one that lacks zeal (v. 15). By contrast Caleb is old (14:10-11) but eager for conflict. The pagan military resistance that intimidates the sons of Joseph (17:16, 18) only goads Caleb to conflict (14:12). What is one group's apprehension is another man's adrenalin.

Observe then how nicely 14:6-15 forms a positive heading and 17:14-18 a negative ending for chapters 14–17. The writer wanted to set the ideal response of faith against the caution, complaint, and hesitancy that arises from fear. The matter was urgent. It was crucial for Israel to respond rightly to the challenge of possessing the land. A Josephite attitude will lead to military inertia (see Judg. 1:27-36), which will in turn create the conditions for religious apostasy (see Judg. 2:6–3:6). Caleb and Ephraim-Manasseh present the models and alternatives for next-generation Israel.[6] It will spell the difference between

---

[5] Woudstra, *Joshua*, 267, points out the contrasting elements.

fidelity and apostasy, between blessing and curse. So if you have read chapters 14–17 as though they comprised an ancient, tedious geography lesson, you have wrongly read them. They are charged with a current that runs through them, the crisis of faith or unbelief. Behind every town he lists and every border he traces the writer is seeking to raise up disciples of Caleb.

Study Questions:

1. Do you find the smaller commands of God, i.e. showing kindness to others, more difficult to obey than the larger commands, i.e. do not commit adultery?

2. Have you ever experienced a lonely faith such as Caleb's? What sustained you during that time?

3. Why is there sometimes confusion as to the power of biblical faith? Is there confusion between a faith based on your feelings, a faith in faith itself, and a faith based on God's Word?

4. Do you find that your perspective of faith takes in God's goodness, responds in gratitude, and finds grace for God's next call?

5. How do you distinguish between biblical faith in Yahweh and 'the power of positive thinking?'

---

[6] Here I am venturing to assume that the material of Joshua functioned as preaching material to the next generation of Israelites (the Judges generation); apologies to those who think it only preached to King Josiah's time.

15

Promise Geography
(Joshua 15)

One Old Testament scholar sees what he calls promise theology[1] as the heart and soul of the Old Testament. By a somewhat loose analogy Joshua 15 could be viewed as promise geography.

I will admit that there seems to be more than a little tedium in reading through Joshua 15. It deals with the inheritance of the tribe of Judah and lovingly traces the boundaries of Judah (vv. 1-12), reports Caleb's victories at Hebron and Debir (vv. 13-20), categorises and lists the various towns belonging to Judah (vv. 21-62), and includes a note of inability or failure (v. 63). Certainly, a text like 'Maon, Carmel, Ziph, Juttah' (v. 55) doesn't exactly stir sermonic juices or suggest warm devotional thoughts. Yet I remain convinced that the apostle was not joking when he said 'all scripture is profitable'; therefore, Joshua 15 must be profitable – and it must be so as it is, without spicing it up with any spirtualising additives.[2]

---

[1] Walter C. Kaiser, Jr., *Toward an Old Testament Theology* (Grand Rapids: Zondervan, 1978).

[2] Cf. Matthew Henry's comments in his preface to chapter 13: 'And therefore we are not to skip over these chapters of hard names as useless and not to be regarded; where God has a mouth to speak and a hand to write we should find an ear to hear and an eye to read; and God give us a heart to profit!' (*Commentary on the Whole Bible*, 6 vols. [New York: Revell, n.d.] 2:71).

Its message may not seem as rich as that of Genesis 22 or
1 Kings 18, but it does have its own useful word.

The Details of God's Promise (15:1-12)

First of all, then, let us stress that chapter 15 deals with the
details of God's promise. Joshua 15 is simply one of the buds
on the tree of Genesis 12 and Genesis 15. The land promise
had long ago been given to Abraham (Gen. 12:6-7; 15:7-21),
was often reaffirmed, and was picked up in Joshua 1; here we
see part of its concrete fulfilment. The reader must remember
that both this chapter and following ones describe in detail
God's gift of the land and that means that every town name
and border point pulsates with excitement. No close-up
description of God's gifts could ever be boring! Perhaps the
contemporary Christian needs some analogy to get a handle
on this.

It is Tuesday morning as I write this. Nothing outstanding
has happened. Two of our boys have had their breakfast – not
significant except that it is another fulfilment of Matthew 6:26.
Today is also garbage pick-up day. We have three bags – more
than usual, but not a big deal. Simply having garbage is a sign
of provision. And even though my wife pulled an irritating
April Fool's prank on me already, she herself is living fulfilment
of Yahweh's covenant promise (Prov. 19:14). Not one of these
details staggers the imagination; but like the boundaries and
towns of Judah they are little incarnations of God's fidelity
and are, therefore, hardly boring.

A Paradigm of Vigorous Faith (15:13-19)

Secondly, verses 13-19 present us with a paradigm of vigorous
faith. In line with Yahweh's command Caleb received his
portion (v. 13). We have already heard Caleb express his
venturesome faith in 14:6-14; however, that passage did not
tell us how Caleb fared when he accosted Hebron.[3] This
passage makes up that deficiency. Caleb not only talked faith

---

[3] Joshua 15:13-19 is parallel to Judges 1:10-15. It is sometimes difficult to
evaluate the various attacks on Hebron and Debir. The attacks in 10:36-39 were
probably prior to Caleb's. However, it is possible that the achievement ascribed to
Joshua in 11:21-22 was actually carried out by Caleb, summary statements, like
11:21-22, being general and not always precise.

but acted in faith, and Yahweh granted him success. This was no measly task – see my exposition of 11:21-22 on the Anakim. Caleb dispossessed these and nailed down Hebron for his clan. The fact that he offered Achsah, his daughter, in marriage to whomever took Debir (v. 16) may indicate that it seemed an insurmountable task.[4] Special incentive for special difficulty. David would later offer an attractive incentive for the one who could reduce the 'impregnable' Jerusalem (1 Chron. 11:5-6). In any case, Othniel captured both Debir and Achsah.[5] Caleb's faith in action becomes a paradigm for Israel; here is the way the initial conquest is to be followed up. Certainly it is a fearful assignment. What could be more formidable than combat with Sheshai, Ahiman, Talmai and their clans? After all, Anak and invincible were supposedly synonomous. But see how the God who promises a secure inheritance enables a clan to obtain it when they are willing to risk obedience to his promise (Exod. 23:30; Deut. 7:22-23).

The Pattern of God's Realism (15:20-63)

Somewhat in line with our first point, we note that this chapter reflects the pattern of God's realism. Karl Gutbrod has made some helpful observations here. Our narrator is no secular history writer but writes as God's messenger with a word to the worshipping community of Israel. The puzzle is how such lists can proclaim the work and power of God to his people. How can this nurture them? Perhaps the solution lies in recognising what may be called biblical realism. God's word is seldom about some bare, purely spiritual, inner abstraction. The God of the Bible tends to be concrete, his gifts tangible and visible. The inheritance he bequeaths is not an idea but boudaries, not thoughts but towns: in a word, *real* estate.

---

[4] John Calvin, *Commentaries on the Book of Joshua*, trans. Henry Beveridge, in vol. 4 of *Calvin's Commentaries*, 22 vols. (reprint ed.; Grand Rapids: Baker, 1981), 206.

[5] Othniel was probably either the younger brother or nephew of Caleb; see C. F. Keil, *Joshua, Judges, Ruth*, Biblical Commentary on the Old Testament (1868; reprint ed.; Grand Rapids: Eerdmans, 1950), 157; Leon J. Wood, 'Othniel', *ZPEB*, 4:552-53. Debir should now probably be identified with Khirbet Rabud, 7.5 miles southwest of Hebron, and not with Tell Beit Mirsim, as formerly held. See Moshe Kochavi, 'Debir (City)', *IDB/S*, 222, and, in detail, Anson F. Rainey, 'Debir', *ISBE* (rev. ed.), 1:901-4.

Yahweh has always been this way – and his infleshment is the great witness to the fact (John 1:1, 14).[6] We western Christians probably need to get a hard grip on this; we need to rediscover the earthiness of God. We must realise that even enjoying the grand act of the kingdom of God will not mean floating as a beeping soul in some sort of spiritual ether but walking around with a resurrection body in new heavens *and a new earth* (cf. Isa. 65–66; Rev. 21–22).

So perhaps we can say that Israel's concrete and tangible inheritance in Canaan[7] is a foreshadowing of our own. Our full possession is in new heavens and a new earth, not in some earthless, fleshless void. Our full expectation ought not to be in dying and going to heaven, as the usual cliché has

---

[6] See the discussion in Karl Gutbrod, *Das Buch vom Lande Gottes,* Die Botschaft des Alten Testaments, 3d ed. (Stuttgart: Calwer, 1965), 115-16.

[7] This chapter certainly reflects the prominence of Judah, but I will leave that aside, hoping to address that theme at a later time from the Book of Judges. I will also not discuss the failure note of verse 63 but will touch on it in the next chapter. However, I do want to append a note on the town list of verses 21-62, particularly in reference to its date.

Judah's towns are listed in four major (geographical) divisions, those in: (1) the Negeb (southland), verses 21-32; (2) the Shephelah (lowland hills to the west), verses 33-47; (3) the hill country, verses 48-60; and (4) the wilderness (to the east), verses 61-62. Some see a total of twelve districts in the whole list, each one usually concluding with the formula, '_____ towns with their villages'. There are twelve districts provided one counts verses 45-47 as one (the usual tally formula is missing) and provided one follows the Septuagint at verse 59 and inserts another district ('Tekoa, Ephrathah, that is, Bethlehem, Peor, Etam, Culom, Tatam, Sores, Carem, Gallim, Baither, and Manach: 11 cities in all with their hamlets', NEB).

A number of scholars hold that this list reflects a much later period (e.g. that of King Jehoshaphat or Josiah). See Otto Kaiser, *Introduction to the Old Testament* (Minneapolis: Augsburg, 1975), 139-40. However, there is need for caution over 'late-dating' the list. The listing of the Philistine cities in verses 45-47 makes more sense if this list originates near the conquest period than if it comes from much later. After several hundred years of Israel or Judah's not controlling these Philistine cities, what later editor would dream of putting them in town list as though they were Judah's? No wonder Frank M. Cross and George Ernest Wright could not explain it (cf. Trent C. Butler, *Joshua,* Word Biblical Commentary [Waco: Word, 1983], 189). But one could understand such a naïve view of Judah's destined territory if it comes from the conquest era before later realities had been set in historical concrete. Moreover, the fact that the Jebusites still lived with Judah in Jerusalem 'to this day' (v. 63) most naturally indicates a date prior to David's capture of Jerusalem (circa 1000 BC) – at least for that note! I do not care to crusade, only to point out that the bulk of the town list can easily be quite early with perhaps a little later editing. See also Kenneth A. Kitchen, 'The Old Testament in Its Context: 3 from Joshua to Solomon', *TSF Bulletin* 61 (Autumn 1971): 7.

it. The New Testament language is that believers, when they die, are 'with the Lord' (2 Cor. 5:8; Phil. 1:23; Luke 23:43). But the New Testament always lifts our eyes and fixes our minds upon the fullness of our hope, the redemption of our bodies on resurrection day at the return of our Lord (Rom. 8:23; Phil. 3:20-21; 1 Thess. 4:16-17; 1 Cor. 15).

STUDY QUESTIONS:

1. How does listing the cities and boarders demonstrate the fulfillment of God's covenant promise?

2. We know that God is able to do more than we can ask or think. Why then does God allow Caleb's victory to be a difficult one? Why not an easier conquest?

3. What insurmountable obstacles have you had to face which required a stronger measure of your faith?

4. How does the incarnation reveal the 'realism' of God?

5. How is Israel's concrete and tangible inheritance in Canaan a foreshadowing of our own?

16

Tragic Trends
(Joshua 16–17)

These chapters describe the tribal allotment of 'the sons of Joseph' (16:1, 4), Ephraim and Manasseh. In spite of some disputed site identifications, their southern boundary (in particular, the southern boundary of Ephraim) can be roughly traced from Jericho up to Bethel, over to lower Beth-Horon, down to Gezer, and on to the Mediterranean (16:2-3.) Michmethah, near Shechem, serves as anchor-point for Ephraim's northern boundary, from which the border 'descended on a sharp diagonal line in each direction, south-east to Jericho and westward along the Wadi Qanah which runs into the Yarkon'[1] (16:6-8). Manasseh's plot was north of Ephraim's; here Ephraim's northern boundary coincided with Manasseh's southern border (17:7-9). Manasseh's northern limits are not sharply defined; they touch Asher's inheritance on the north and Issachar's on the east (17:10).[2]

---

[1] Yohanan Aharoni, *The Land of the Bible: A Historical Geography*, rev. and enl. (Philadelphia: Westminster, 1979), 257. See also Yohanan Aharoni and Michael Avi-Yonah, *The Macmillan Bible Atlas*, rev. ed. (New York: Macmillan, 1977), 52, or *The New Layman's Bible Commentary* (Grand Rapids: Zondervan, 1979), 329.

[2] For a readable, useful description of Ephraim and Manasseh's territory, see George Adam Smith, *The Historical Geography of the Holy Land,* 22d ed. (London: Hodder and Stoughton, n.d.), chapter 16.

Again, this is not merely another careful land survey. Certain notations, anecdotes, and repetitions in these chapters call for attention. Some of these items augur ill for Israel's future.

A Reminder of Yahweh's Ways (16:1-4)

We receive a reminder of Yahweh's ways in the first verses of chapter 16. In verses 1-4 a reference to the sons of Joseph opens and closes the section; in the latter instance, they are defined as Manasseh and Ephraim (v. 4). This was the order of birth; Manasseh was the older of Joseph's sons. However, the writer proceeds to describe Ephraim's territory before Manasseh's allotment. 'He then (v. 5) calls attention, implicitly to be sure, to God's sovereign arrangement which had given Ephraim the priority.'[3]

Someone may object that this is too subtle. But I doubt it. Not if one senses that Genesis 48 is the baggage behind Joshua 16–17. In fact God's arrangement is very subtle in Genesis 48 – at least at first. Joseph brings his two sons Manasseh and Ephraim (Gen. 48:1; note the order of birth) before his aged father Jacob. But when Jacob first refers to them he vows that 'Ephraim and Manasseh shall be mine, as Reuben and Simeon are' (v. 5). This is a subtle switch, but deliberate. For when Joseph presents the lads for Jacob's blessing he places Manasseh, the older, opposite Jacob's right hand – naturally, and Ephraim opposite Jacob's left (v. 14). But blind, old Jacob crossed his arms and placed his right hand on Ephraim's head, giving him priority! Joseph knew that was not right, so he tried to straighten out his father's tangle (vv. 17-18), but Jacob assured his son that his hands knew what they were doing (v. 19). Jacob's blessing ran: 'When a blessing is pronounced in Israel, men shall use your names and say, God make you like Ephraim and Manasseh' (v. 20, NEB). To this the writer appends the note: 'So he put Ephraim before Manasseh.'

That is what Joshua 16–17 does. The writer knows their order of birth (16:4) but he puts Ephraim (16:5-10) before Manasseh (17:1-13). He doesn't ring any bells about it; it's just

---

[3] Marten H. Woudstra, *The Book of Joshua*, the New International Commentary on the Old Testament (Grand Rapids: Eerdmans, 1981), 259.

a reminder, another hint of Yahweh's strange ways. How often the divine way reverses the conventions of men, overthrows the human canon of what ought to be. That's why the God of the Bible is so stimulating and refreshing. He is never the prisoner of what fallen man regards as normal. Again and again he turns human standards on their heads, causing us to wonder and cheer. Without this God who ignores our proprieties, most of us would have no hope.

> My brothers, think what sort of people you are, whom God has called. Few of you are men of wisdom, by any human standard; few are powerful or highly born. Yet, to shame the wise, God has chosen what the world counts folly, and to shame what is strong, God has chosen what the world counts weakness. He has chosen things low and contemptible, mere nothings, to overthrow the existing order. And so there is no place for human pride in the presence of God. (1 Cor. 1:26-29, NEB)

> Listen, my dear brothers: it was those who are poor according to the world that God chose, to be rich in faith and to be the heirs to the kingdom which he promised to those who love him. (James 2:5, JB)

The same motive may also explain why Judah's lot (ch. 15) is mentioned before those of the other tribes, even Ephraim and Manasseh. It may well be a reflection of Jacob's prophecy in Genesis 49:8-12, especially that the ruler's staff was to be planted between Judah's feet. Yet that, too, seems to be one of the Lord's twists. Judah was not the oldest (Gen. 29:31-35), nor the one favoured with the birthright (see 1 Chron. 5:1-2). If you have a warm spot for him because he protected Benjamin (Gen. 43:8-10; 44:16-34), you must realise he is the same fellow who didn't mind bedding down with a Canaanite harlot (for all he knew; Gen. 38). So Judah will have the royal primacy – not because of birth, favouritism, or virtue – simply by sovereignty because God is not imprisoned either by Roberts' or our 'Rules of Order'. And that is the reason to adore him.

A Pleading of Yahweh's Word (17:3-6)

Secondly, in the case of Zelophedad's daughters, we observe a pleading of Yahweh's word. The background for the incident comes from Numbers 27:1-11 (and 36:1-12). Zelophedad died having no sons. So his five daughters appeal to Moses, asking that what would have been their father's land inheritance not be diverted to the nearest male relative but that they, his daughters, be granted his inheritance, uncustomary as this might seem.[4] Moses referred the matter to Yahweh, who decided in their favour. In this request Zelophedad's girls declared their faith. As John Calvin put it:

> Inasmuch as they would not have been so anxious about the succession, if God's promise had not been just as much a matter of certainty to them as if they were at this moment demanding to be put in possession of it. They had not yet entered the land, nor were their enemies conquered; yet, relying on the testimony of Moses, they prosecute their suit as if the tranquil possession of their rights were to be accorded them that very day.[5]

Their follow-up here in Joshua 17 indicates the same sort of implicit faith. They remind Eleazar and Joshua that 'Yahweh commanded Moses to give us an inheritance among our brothers.' As with Caleb (14:6-12) there is boldness to request what Yahweh had already promised, a forthrightness to plead Yahweh's past word.

It is here that Mahlah and her sisters may be our school mistresses to bring us to Christ. Numerous Christians lack the boldness, assurance, and confidence to lay hold of God's provisions. We are like folk who enter a shop or store, gather what we need, and find no one minding the cash register at the moment. However, there is a bell at the counter and a sign, 'Ring bell for service.' Frequently we are hesitant to ring the bell for all sorts of foolish reasons: for example, they will think I'm impatient; I hate to appear demanding; it will probably irritate the clerk if I interrupt whatever he or she is doing. Somehow we can hardly imagine that the shopkeeper

---

[4] See Gordon J. Wenham, *Numbers*, Tyndale Old Testament Commentaries (Leicester: Inter-Varsity, 1981), 191-93.

[5] John Calvin, *Commentaries on the Four Last Books of Moses*, trans. Charles William Bingham, in vol. 3 of *Calvin's Commentaries*, 22 vols. (reprint ed.; Grand Rapids: Baker, 1981), 4:256.

provided the bell because he actually wants his customers to use it!

That is precisely the point the writer of Hebrews seeks to make. If Jesus, the Son of God, is our great and sympathetic high priest at the right hand of God, what ought we to do? 'Let us then with confidence draw near to the throne of grace that we may ... find grace to help in time of need' (Heb. 4:16). If Jesus the Tempted One is God's provision for us in our temptations, what should we do? Why, come to him, use him, claim what God has supplied. If God has provided a throne of grace, then let us by all means draw near so that we may find grace for help at just the right time. But let the daughters of Zelophedad teach you not to waver bashfully about laying hold of God's promised provisions.

A Deviation from Yahweh's Program (17:7-13)

We do not need to wait until Judges 1 to hear a degree of failure in regard to the conquest. We have it already in Joshua. Indeed these chapters show that Israel permitted themselves a deviation from Yahweh's program relating to the conquest. Such is clear from the repeated notes of failure. If we cheat for a moment and go back to include chapter 15, then we find three notes of failure, each appearing at the end of accounts of the tribal allotments.

> As for the Jebusites, the residents of Jerusalem, the sons of Judah were not able to dispossess; so the Jebusites continue to live with the sons of Judah in Jerusalem to this day [15:63].

> But they did not dispossess the Canaanites who live in Gezer; so the Canaanites live among Ephraim to this day; then they were put to forced labor [16:10].

> But the sons of Manasseh were not able to possess these cities; the Canaanites were determined to live in this land. Yet when the sons of Israel became strong they put the Canaanites to forced labor and did not thoroughly dispossess them [17:12-13].

The reader will see an intensification of blame in these notes. First, Judah's inability; then Ephraim's failure in regard to one city and, evidently, settling for the Canaanites' subservience rather than expulsion; finally, Manasseh's massive inability or failure to control a number of strategic locations, along with their preference (even when they became strong) for resident Canaanite slaves than for vanquished enemies.

Such accommodation and laxity plainly contradicted Yahweh's clear directions (Exod. 23:23-33; 34:11-16; Deut. 7:1-6). He had told Israel that the residents of Canaan 'must not live in your land' (Exod. 23:33); he had commanded Israel to destroy them completely and to show them no grace (Deut. 7:2). Spiritual emergency required violent holiness (see. Deut. 7:6 in context). The cancer of Baal worship would surely infect Israel unless the most radical surgery removed it (Exod. 23:32-33; Deut. 7:4). There was something strangely catching in Canaan's credo that the world moved by the sexual prowess of Baal (and his disciples) rather than by the almighty hand of Yahweh.

True, Yahweh had informed Israel that there would be a gradual aspect to the conquest:

> I will not drive them out from before you in one year, lest the land become desolate and the wild beasts multiply against you. Little by little I will drive them out from before you, until you are increased and possess the land [Exod. 23:29-30, RSV; see also Deut. 7:22-23].

But here in Joshua, Ephraim and Manasseh show that by their compromise they have already begun to lose this vision (16:10; 17:12-13); for the failure notes clearly reveal that, after a period of inability or unwillingness, the time came when Israel became dominant, since they made forced labourers out of the Canaanites. They had power to expel them at Yahweh's direction but chose to retain them for their own advantage. As Calvin saw:

> But another crime still less pardonable was committed when, having it in their power easily to destroy all, they not only were slothful in executing the command of God, but, induced by filthy lucre, they preserved those alive whom God had doomed to destruction.[6]

Here was the deviation from Yahweh's program. Let the contemporary Christian, however, be slow to pick up the first stone. For we frequently repeat Israel's pattern. Israel evidently had functioned fairly well in the initial onslaught of the conquest, in the united push under Joshua. With the major crisis past, the time came for tribes to complete the conquest, remaining faithful in Yahweh's little-by-little work (Exod. 23:30). Somehow, we relish the call for heroism but not that for durability. We find being faithful in little more annoying than satisfying. No wonder Jesus warns us that those who at first are most ecstatic over him may only 'endure for a while' (Mark 4:16-17). The Christian's faith is not so much proved by his courage in a sudden crisis as by his faithfulness in daily plodding. (See the exposition of my second point on Joshua 13.)

In Joshua 16–17 Ephraim and Manasseh's failure brings no immediate dire consequences. We must wait for the Book of Judges for that. Here it is mere obedience, if there is such a thing.

A Discontent with Yahweh's Gift (17:14-18)
Finally, there appears in 17:14-18 a discontent with Yahweh's gift.[7] Though there are some obscure details in this passage, the primary point is clear. The Joseph tribes (Ephraim and Manasseh) complain that they have been given but 'one lot and one portion' though they are a 'numerous people'. (This last phrase is used three times in these verses, once by the tribes and twice by Joshua, who picked it up.) Naturally, they piously attribute their numerical strength to the fact that 'Yahweh has blessed me' (v. 14).[8]

Joshua's first reply (v. 15) directs them to go up to 'the forest area[9] and clear out a place for yourselves there in the land

---

[6] John Calvin, *Commentaries on the Book of Joshua*, trans. Henry Beveridge, in vol. 4 of *Calvin's Commentaries*, 22 vols. (reprint ed.; Grand Rapids: Baker, 1981), 217.

[7] I have already discussed the function of this section in connection with 14:6-15. See comments on that passage.

[8] The Joseph tribes may well have expected Joshua's ready assent to their implied request since Joshua himself was of the tribe of Ephraim (Num. 13:8).

[9] I assume that the forest area denotes some perhaps less settled portion within the 'hill country of Ephraim'. On this view, the Joseph tribes may mean in verse 16

of the Perizzites and the Rephaim'. Since, as you say, the hill country of Ephraim is too confined for you, and since, as you say, you are a numerous people, then nothing should stop you from clearing out more living space in that enemy territory.

The Josephites' response discloses their true attitude. They may be saying that the hill country, whether cleared or not, 'is not enough for us' (lit., 'it will not be found for us'). Most construe the clause in this way.[10] A case can be made, however, for 'will (can-) not be acquired by us'.[11] If so, they are even despairing of an extensive hold on the hill country, let alone the plain so ably patrolled by Canaanite chariots. Joshua's retort in verse 18 fits better with the latter view: 'For the hill country will be yours; sure, it's forest – and you'll clear it....' He seems to respond to a 'can't' rather than a 'not enough'. So Joseph's sons don't push into the Plain of Esdraelon to the north where the Canaanites could use their 'tanks' against mere tribal infantry. Yet they are a numerous people – and 'one lot' is hardly enough (v. 14). So there is discontent with Yahweh's gift.

We may think that Joshua's answer in verses 17-18 is just so much shallow pep talk. It is as if he says, 'Sure, the Canaanites have a meat grinder in the Plain of Esdraelon (Jezreel); but that's all right; run into it and see what you can do.' But that misreads Joshua.

It is difficult to translate Joshua's words in verses 17-18, primarily because he uses the Hebrew particle *ki* five times in verse 18, and it is hard to know just how to construe some of these. If allowed a colloquial corruption or two I would suggest: 'You are a numerous people; you have great power; you will not have (only) one lot; for the hill country will be yours; sure, it's forest – and you'll clear it out and its borders will be yours; indeed, you will dispossess the Canaanites; sure, they have

---

that the hill country would be insufficient even if they did clear out additional area within it.

[10] E.g. NASB, RSV, NEB, NIV; also C. F. Keil, *Joshua, Judges, Ruth*, Biblical Commentary on the Old Testament (1868; reprint ed.; Grand Rapids: Eerdmans, 1950), 184, and Francis Brown, Samuel R. Driver, and Charles A. Briggs, eds., *A Hebrew and English Lexicon of the Old Testament* (Oxford: Clarendon, 1907), 594.

[11] See *Gesenius' Hebrew and Chaldee Lexicon*, trans. S. P. Tregelles (reprint ed.; Grand Rapids: Eerdmans, 1949), 499; and George Bush, *Notes, Critical and Practical, on the Book of Joshua* (Chicago: Henry A. Sumner, 1881), 170.

iron chariots; sure, they're strong.' Joshua's answer is not a piece of theology that refuses to look at or empathise with the obstacles God's people face. It is rather a theology informed by a word of God that had already addressed precisely this situation:

> You may say in your heart, 'These nations outnumber me; how shall I be able to dispossess them?' Do not be afraid of them; remember how Yahweh your God dealt with Pharaoh and all Egypt, the great ordeals your own eyes have seen, the signs and wonders, the mighty hand and outstretched arm with which Yahweh your God has brought you out. So will Yahweh your God deal with all the peoples whom you fear to face.... Do not be afraid of them, for Yahweh your God is among you, a God who is great and terrible. Little by little Yahweh your God will destroy these nations before you [Deut. 7:17-22, JB].

> When you go to war against your enemies and see horses and chariots and an army greater than your own, you must not be afraid of them; Yahweh your God is with you, who brought you out of the land of Egypt [Deut. 20:1, JB].

Ephraim and Manasseh's complaint began with discontent for Yahweh's gift; but our passage shows a deeper problem: distrust of Yahweh's adequacy. Not that God did not know their fears; Deuteronomy 7 and 20 show he knew them well. But Ephraim and Manasseh must remember who Yahweh is! He is the God who brought you up out of the land of Egypt, who bludgeoned Pharaoh to his knees, the great and terrible God who is in the midst of you. Once you see Yahweh, Perizzite swords and Canaanite chariots lose their dread. This is not merely the problem of two tribes but of God's people in all ages. In spite of our professions, we are in fact barely supernaturalists. Again and again our Lord has to remind us that God is not the prisoner of human odds, that his promises are at least as real as the iron plating on Canaanite chariots, but that we will see little of his power until we venture out into the way of obedience, until we trust his promise enough to walk in it.

STUDY QUESTIONS:

1. God seems to be unconventional in his ways. Does this make you adore him more or questions his ways?

2. How might your prayer life be strengthened if you prayed more deeply with boldness for his promises? Are you bold in your prayers?

3. How can you avoid not letting down and finishing the task when there is no immediate crisis?

4. Do you find yourself trust God with, "Yes Lord, but...?"

5. Is it harder to trust God in the hard times or in the easy times?

17

Lots of Lots
(Joshua 18–19)

Since these chapters are loaded with details, the following outline of their contents may be helpful:

The assembly at the sanctuary, 18:1-10
    Opportunity: the land 'subdued', 18:1
    Crisis: the people 'slack', 18:2-3
    Plan: the land 'written up', 18:4-7
    Execution: the land 'portioned out', 18:8-10
The lots for the tribes, 18:11–19:48
    Inheritance of Benjamin, 18:11-28
        Boundaries, 18:11-20
        Towns, 18:21-28
    Inheritance of Simeon, 19:1-9
    Inheritance of Zebulun, 19:10-16
    Inheritance of Issachar, 19:17-23
    Inheritance of Asher, 19:24-31
    Inheritance of Naphtali, 19:32-39
    Inheritance of Dan, 19:40-48
The reward for the leader, 19:49-51

Again, a contemporary Christian reader of Joshua 18–19 would have to confess that he is not interested in lots. However, I would again insist that all Scripture is profitable and that instructive notes ring in these chapters as well.

143

A New Day (18:1)

Israel's assembling and setting up the tabernacle at Shiloh, hints at the dawn of a new day. Shiloh was about ten miles northeast of Bethel, thirty miles north of Jerusalem, in the tribal territory of Ephraim. Shiloh seems to have been the primary centre of Israelite worship during the pre-monarchic period (Josh. 18:1; 21:2, 22:9, 12; Judg. 18:31; 21:12, 19; 1 Sam. 1–2). This was a new situation. The day would come, Moses had told Israel (Deut. 12:1-15), when Yahweh would choose a place in the land where he was to be worshipped, a place where sacrifices were to be offered and sacrificial meals enjoyed. The semilaxity of the wilderness period would cease when God brought them into their inheritance and gave them rest in the land. Here they were to worship faithfully (turning away from the many Canaanite holy spots around them to this one worship centre), joyfully ('and you shall rejoice before Yahweh your God, you and your sons and your daughters and your male and female servants, as well as the Levite who lives within your town gates'), and securely (for Yahweh would give them rest from enemies). Now Yahweh's dwelling place was erected at Shiloh, where he had caused his name to dwell (cf. Jer. 7:12). 'The desert did not provide the paradigm for the settled life in the promised land.'[1] Yahweh's intention was for his people to worship him in fidelity, joy, and security.

Shiloh may have marked such a new day, but it was not the final new day. Zechariah saw it and was glad, the time when Yahweh would 'enable us to serve him without fear in holiness and righteousness before him all our days' (Luke 1:74-75, NIV). Many of our brothers and sisters long for the new day when they can worship and serve God without fear. But already with Israel we have a clear glimpse of God's intention for us – to worship him faithfully, joyfully, securely.

A Constant Concern (18:5-7)

Secondly, our writer betrays a constant concern to stress that all Israel, that all twelve tribes receive their share of the land inheritance (18:5-7). As Marten H. Woudstra points out,

---

[1] P. C. Craigie, *The Book of Deuteronomy*, The New International Commentary on the Old Testament (Grand Rapids: Eerdmans, 1976), 218. I realise the reference to Deuteronomy 12 opens a can of critical worms, but they can just crawl around for now.

This is not needless redundancy but proceeds from the writer's thematic interest in the twelve-tribe scheme and in the unity of Israel as it participates equally in the Conquest (cf. 1:12-18) and as it shares alike in the distribution of the promised land.[2]

We last saw it in chapter 13; here again is this careful passion to account for all Israel. So, our writer runs us through the tribal math again. 'Now,' he says, 'there are seven portions for these seven remaining tribes (18:5a), though Judah (one tribe) is already placed in the south and Joseph (one and a half tribes) in the north (18:5b). Please remember that Levi (one tribe) inherits priesthood instead of real estate (18:7a) and that two and a half tribes have already received their lots east of the Jordan.' This emphasis comes via Joshua's speech, but it is clearly an emphasis the writer wants to make (cf. ch. 22).

Christian believers can profit from this perspective. We always face the temptation of thinking that we are elite rather than elect, of thinking that, after all, our own particular Christian ghetto is swankier than the others, or of simply losing sight of the fact that other believers share the same Father's wealth. The New Testament is adamant about this. 'Because out of his fullness [see 1:14] we *all* have received, even grace on top of grace' (John 1:16). 'For by one Spirit we *all* were baptised into one body – Jews or Greeks, slaves or free, and *all* have been given one Spirit to drink' (1 Cor. 12:13). 'But to *each one* of us grace was given in line with the measure of Christ's gift' (Eph. 4:7). The Scriptures are not denying Christian diversity, only rebuking Christian snobbery. All God's people matter to him; each one is his heir.

A Dangerous Laxity
We hear the keynote, however, of chapters 18–19 when Joshua accuses the seven tribes of developing a dangerous laxity toward the task of possessing the land. 'How long will you continue to show yourselves slack about going in to possess the land that Yahweh the God of your fathers has given you?' (18:3). The verbal idea of being slack is a participial form and

[2] Marten H. Woudstra, *The Book of Joshua*, The New International Commentary on the Old Testament (Grand Rapids: Eerdmans, 1981), 270-71.

indicates a persisting action or attitude. It comes from the same root as the verb in 1:5, where Yahweh promises Joshua, 'I will not let go of you' (or, 'I will not drop you'). Here Israel is in danger of letting go, of dropping the call to possess the gift of God.

Now was the crucial time. 'The land was subdued before them' (v. 1). Here was their opportunity. While the land was subdued (Hebrew, *kabash*) they must press on to possess (Hebrew, *yarash*) it (v. 3). With the backbone of Canaanite resistance presently broken, these tribes must follow up this advantage and nail down the land (i.e. permanently occupy it). But here they remain – letting the opportunity slip away.

Joshua did what he could to get Israel on with it. They were to select three men from each of the seven tribes in question; these twenty-one men were to case out the land and write up a description of it. Then Joshua would cast lots for these tribes and portion out their inheritances to them (vv. 3-7). Perhaps that would shove them out of their sluggishness.

Verse 3 reflects the tension of much believing experience, ancient Israelite and contemporary Christian. Yahweh has promised the land and yet it must be possessed. It is Yahweh's gift and yet that does not cancel human responsibility. Yahweh's promises are intended not as sedatives but as stimulants. God does not want us to swallow his promises but to seize them. Such is the apostle's 'theo-logic' in 2 Peter 1:3ff. Peter exclaims that 'His divine power has granted to us everything pertaining to life and godliness' and that 'He has granted to us His precious and magnificent promises' (NASB). Then he concludes: 'Now *for this very reason* also, applying *all diligence*, in your faith supply moral excellence, and in your moral excellence, knowledge', and so on (NASB; emphasis added). God's gifts are not meant to tame but to arouse God's people.

H. L. Ellison has probably assessed Israel's slackness correctly:

> The slackness blamed by Joshua (3) may well have been due to an unwillingness to settle down. It was fine to have a 'promised land,' but the reality showed the need for learning new skills and engaging in hard work. That is for many the disappointing side

of God's gifts; they are always given that we may serve the better. Even his rest is linked with a yoke (Matt. 11:28-30).[3]

For application, see the previous chapter, and my comments on deviation from Yahweh's program.

A Necessary Authority

Fourthly, we can note how carefully Joshua places this land division under a necessary authority. Three times we read that after the twenty-one men write up the land, the lot will be cast for the seven tribes 'before Yahweh' (18:6, 8, 10), that is, before Yahweh's presence at the tabernacle in Shiloh.

> The transaction was a solemn one, and he would have it so performed as that the tribes should look upon their possessions, as established to them by divine authority.[4]

Though this seems perfunctory enough to us, it was nevertheless necessary. There could be no end of complaint, quarrelling, or discontent unless the tribes were assured that their lot was determined by the hand of God, that their territory was theirs by Yahweh's decision. The heart of the matter differs little for the Christian, though it may seldom involve real estate. Only as I am convinced that 'my times are in thy hand' (Ps. 31:15 – see v. 13 for what those times can be like!) and that Yahweh really does hold my lot (cf. Ps. 16:5), can I be kept from bitterness and discontent. There is, by a strange chemistry, something oddly consoling when I realise in a fresh way that my present lot is what my Lord has intended for me.

---

[3] H. L. Ellison, *Scripture Union Bible Study Books: Joshua – 2 Samuel* (Grand Rapids: Eerdmans, 1966), 17. William Blaikie (*The Book of Joshua,* The Expositor's Bible [Cincinnati: Jennings and Graham, n.d.], 315) makes a similar point: 'Many of them would have been content to jog on carelessly as they had been doing in the desert, in a sort of confused jumble, and to forage about, here and there, as the case might be, in pursuit of the necessaries of life. Their listlessness was provoking. They knew that the divine plan was quite different, that each tribe was to have a territory of its own, and that measures ought to be taken at once to settle the boundaries of each tribe. But they were taking no steps for this purpose; they were content with social hugger-mugger.'

[4] George Bush, *Notes, Critical and Practical, on the Book of Joshua* (Chicago: Henry A. Sumner, 1881), 174.

A Completed Allotment

Fifthly, chapters 18–19 show us a completed allotment. Whether these seven tribes will overcome their laxity and press their current advantage by cleaning out their local inheritances is not yet clear, but Joshua has done what he could by prodding them and assigning their various lots.

We need not give a close treatment of the geographical-topographical details; the reader may find these elsewhere.[5] However, we should note the general location of these tribal lots.

Benjamin received the hill country south of Ephraim and north of Judah (18:11), a section twenty-six miles long east to west and twelve miles wide north to south.[6] The description of Benjamin's inheritance is about twice as long (18:11-28) as that of any of the remaining six tribes, though it is difficult to say precisely how that may be significant.

Simeon is unique in that its inheritance consists of towns within the southwestern section of Judah's territory (19:1-9). Zebulun's portion (19:10-16) was in southern Galilee with Asher on the northwest, Naphtali on the northeast, Issachar on the southeast, and Manasseh on the southwest, where the Wadi Kishon formed the border.[7] Issachar (19:17-23) settled at the east end of the Valley of Jezreel (Esdraelon) with the Mount Gilboa range to the south and the hills of Lower Galilee on the north.[8]

Asher's area (19:24-31) stretched all the way from Mount Carmel in the south to Sidon in the north, from the Mediterranean on the west to the western slopes of the Galilean hills on the east. Naphtali's lot (19:32-39) is not easy to trace, but in general lay between the area of Mount Tabor in the south and the River Litani in the north; on the east it touched the upper Jordan River; hence it covered the greater portion of eastern and central Galilee.[9] Dan's original territory

---

[5] For maps, see *The New Layman's Bible Commentary* (Grand Rapids: Zondervan, 1979), 330-33. For site locations, see Woudstra, *Joshua,* 276-96, and Yohanan Aharoni, *The Land of the Bible: A Historical Geography*, rev. and enl. (Philadelphia: Westminster, 1979), 248-62.

[6] Fred E. Young, 'Benjamin', *Wycliffe Bible Encyclopedia*, 2 vols. (Chicago: Moody, 1975), 1:218.

[7] Arthur E. Cundall, 'Zebulun', *IBD*, 3:1677.

[8] Arthur E. Cundall, 'Issachar', *IBD*, 2:720.

[9] Aapeli A. Saarisalo, 'Naphtali', *ISBE* (rev. ed.), 3:490, and Arthur E. Cundall, 'Naphtali', *IBD*, 2:1053.

(19:40-48) lay west of Benjamin's with Ephraim on the north and Judah on the south.

Let me enter a word about the date of these chapters (see also the discussion on ch. 15).

It has become a scholarly shibboleth to hold that these town lists and border descriptions arose from a time later than the conquest era and have been placed here by the editor(s) of Joshua as though they had arisen in the time of Joshua (when in fact they come from the time of Jehoshaphat, Josiah, or the exile).[10] There are hints, however, that the lists are early, dating from the conquest and settlement periods. Adding parenthetical explanations of old place names (e.g. 18:13, 28) suggests the original document(s) was (or were) quite old. If these lists reflect only later historical realities, it is difficult to understand Ekron in Philistia being allotted to Dan (19:43), since there is no evidence that Ekron was ever conquered (other than the temporary taking [Judg. 1:18]).[11] Certainly no later writer aware of (later) historical fact would have dreamed of extending Asher's territory as far as Sidon (19:28; cf. Judg. 1:31), for Sidon was always beyond the pale of Israelite conquest. But such naïveté (as thinking Asher should occupy Sidon) would be perfectly in place at an early date before Israel's failure to occupy all the land became clear. I do not deny that there are problems in these lists; for example, the tallies of towns in 19:15, 30, 38 do not match up with the towns mentioned in the respective lists. But there is no need to hold that these lots are later constructions retrojected into the Book of Joshua as though they arose at that time.

An Eloquent Witness (19:49-50)

There is, lastly, an eloquent witness to hear at the end of chapter 19. I refer to the note about Joshua's inheritance in verses 49-50: 'So they finished distributing the land by its boundaries, and the sons of Israel gave an inheritance among them to Joshua the son of Nun. On the authority of Yahweh they gave it to him – the town he asked for, Timnath-serah, in

---

[10] See the helpful survey of research provided by Trent C. Butler, *Joshua*, Word Biblical Commentary (Waco: Word, 1983), 142-44.

[11] Woudstra, *Joshua*, 294 n.

the hill country of Ephraim; so he rebuilt the town and lived
in it.'

Karl Gutbrod, glancing back over chapters 14–19, has
rightly stated:

> The territorial description of the west Jordan tribes stands in a
> striking framework. It begins with the granting of an inheritance
> to Caleb and ends with the granting of such to Joshua.[12]

Hence the whole account of the land distribution (for the
western tribes) must be held together. It is true that the opening
(18:1) and closing (19:51) references to Shiloh bind together
particularly chapters 18 and 19,[13] but this does not negate the
fact that chapters 14–19 form a larger unit (compare 14:1 and
19:51a). Indeed one can now detect an overall arrangement in
these chapters. I have already pointed out a contrast between
Caleb and the Joseph tribes at the beginning and end,
respectively, of 14:6–17:18. We can also observe the negative
view of the seven tribes at the first of chapters 18–19 (18:3ff.)
and the positive counterpart in Joshua at the end (19:49-50).
The framework is this:

Caleb, 14:6-15	positive
Joseph tribes, 17:14-18	negative
Seven tribes, 18:1-10	negative
Joshua, 19:49-50	positive

The contrasts and the overall framework with its focus on
Caleb and Joshua cannot help but drive us back to Numbers
13–14. There, of the twelve spies, only Caleb and Joshua were
willing to gamble on the sure promise of God to overcome
Canaan (Num. 13:30; 14:6-9). Unfortunately, the majority
report had been contagious. However, Yahweh promised

---

[12] Karl Gutbrod, *Das Buch vom Lande Gottes*, Die Botschaft des Alten Testaments,
3d ed. (Stuttgart: Calwer, 1965), 126; his discussion of verses 49-50 is useful. See
also Woudstra, *Joshua*, 296.

[13] C. F. Keil, *Joshua, Judges, Ruth*, Biblical Commentary on the Old Testament
(1868; reprint ed.; Grand Rapids: Eerdmans, 1950), 208.

that his remnant of two believers would in fact enter the land (Num. 14:24, 30, 38) while the rest would die off for their unbelief. At that time Yahweh had doubtless given specific assurances of an inheritance to both Caleb and Joshua (see Caleb's words in Joshua 14:6, 'about you and me').[14] Hence Joshua's inheritance, no less than Caleb's, is 'on the authority of Yahweh' (19:50) and is in perfect line with 'the word that Yahweh spoke' (14:6).

So 19:49-50 is no useless tailpiece. Though the notes are not visible in the text, it's really music. It is simply 'Great Is Thy Faithfulness' (Lam. 3:23) in a different key. It is a standing witness to the fact that the majority may be neither faithful nor right (Num. 13–14). It is a witness to the fact that Yahweh keeps his promises (Num. 14:24, 30), even if he must preserve his two faithful men from Anakim, chariots, and high water to do so.

There are lots of lots in chapters 14–10. As they begin with Caleb, so they close with Joshua. What a fulfilment of Numbers 13–14! There is far more theology in Hebron and Timnath-serah than one usually hears.

Study Questions:

1. Do you believe that our 21st Century churches are places where God is worshipped faithfully, joyfully and securely?

2. In what ways do you see Christian snobbery today?

3. The Puritans often used the term 'sloth' to describe a sinful spiritual laziness on the part of the believer. How does such sloth affect the life and effectiveness of the believer?

4. Do you recognize that your 'lot in life' is really by the hand of God?

5. How might the allotment to Joshua be an encouragement to Israel? To you?

---

14 Bush, *Joshua*, 181.

18

Final Provisions
(Joshua 20–21)

The business of Israel's inheritance is nearly complete, but the writer has several finishing touches to include. These chapters also appear to major on mundane matters and dreary details. But to think so only means we haven't heard their witness. Let us then listen.

Yahweh's Justice (20:1-9)

The Justice of Yahweh's Justice
Yahweh takes the initiative and commands Joshua and Israel to follow through on instructions given to Moses for setting aside cities of refuge (see Num. 35:9-34; Deut. 4:41-43; 19:1-13). Such cities were to serve as temporary and/or ongoing places of asylum for those guilty of (in our nomenclature) unintentional manslaughter; they were a provision for the one who wipes out a human life 'unintentionally and without designing to do so' (v. 3). If two men, for example, go into the forest to cut wood and one fellow's axe head flies off and hits and kills the other, that man does not deserve to die since he did not maliciously, deliberately, or intentionally cause the death of his friend (Deut. 19:5-6). God's law and rule takes note of the motives and intents in such cases. A man without a

murderer's heart should not suffer a murderer's punishment (for which see Num. 35:30-31; Deut. 19:11-13).[1]

The Accessibility of Yahweh's Justice

The danger in such cases was that the 'redeemer of blood' (Josh. 20:3, 5), the near relative of the slain person charged with maintaining family rights, might – in the heat of the moment – slay the manslayer before the facts of the case could be known and dealt with properly. So vindictive vengeance rather than proper retribution would win the day, and injustice would be added to tragedy. For this reason the accessibility of Yahweh's justice was crucial. Hence six cities of refuge were selected, three on each side of the Jordan, with one in the north, one in the middle area, and one in the south in each set. West of the Jordan, from north to south, were Kedesh, Shechem, and Hebron; east of the Jordan, from north to south, were Golan, Ramoth-gilead, and Bezer (vv. 7-8). The roads were to be prepared (Deut. 19:3) and the cities strategically located so that safety for the unintentional killer was near. In one of these cities he was safe from the immediate wrath of the redeemer of blood until the case could be properly decided. The very number and location of the cities show how available God's justice was meant to be and how practical his ways are.

The Values of Yahweh's Justice

The provision of the cities of refuge also reflects the values of Yahweh's justice. The chapter breathes the sanctity of human life – both the manslayer's and the dead man's. We can clearly see that the concern with these cities assumes the preciousness of the unintentional manslayer's life. But we may not so clearly see that the slain man's life is presumed sacred as well. For the city of refuge is not only a place of

[1] This is not to say that any killer could run to a city of refuge, claim he killed unintentionally, and be home free. After the killer was admitted to the city of refuge, he had to 'stand before the assembly for judgment' (v. 6; cf. also v. 9). Whether this assembly consisted of representatives in or near the city of refuge or possibly refers to officials from the killer's home town is unclear (cf. Num. 35:24-25). But only after the court was convinced that the killer had not acted deliberately or out of hatred and enmity was his ongoing sojourn in the city of refuge approved. The cities of refuge were in no way a legal means of escaping justice, much as that pattern may be the vogue today.

safety for the manslayer but also of exile. He enjoys protection but also suffers penalty. He cannot – assuming the case was decided in his favour, verse 6a – return to his home town and resume normal life; he must stay in the city of refuge until the death of the current high priest (v. 6b). Nor can he leave the bounds of that city, for, if he does, he is fair game for the slain man's relative (Num. 35:26-28). As Trent C. Butler says, the city is 'at the same time refuge and prison'.[2] Such is the costliness of destroying human life; even when that life is taken unintentionally the consequences of that wrong must be carried. Life made in God's image always remains exceedingly sacred (Gen. 9:6).[3]

The Satisfaction of Yahweh's Justice

The unintentional taking of life was so serious that there could be no release from one's stint in the city of refuge – except by the death of the high priest (v. 6). Now the hermeneutical ice may be thin here, but I suggest that the manslayer's release upon the high priest's death may point to the satisfaction of Yahweh's justice.

Numbers 35, especially verses 31-34, provides more detail on this point since Joshua 20 is quite condensed. Apparently, in the case of some crimes where capital punishment was the penalty, one could ransom his life by substituting a monetary compensation – but such an option was not available to a murderer (Num. 35:31). The reason is because blood pollutes the land, and only the blood of the blood-shedder can atone for the land; the only acceptable payment is the murder's own life; only that will purge away the pollution and cleanse the land of defilement. That is the only satisfaction of justice in such a case.

But a similar stipulation holds in the case of unintentional manslaughter. After all, blood pollutes the land, whether that blood was shed via murder or manslaughter. So, 'you are not to accept a ransom-payment for one who has fled to his city of refuge, allowing him to go back and live in the land before the

---

[2] Trent C. Butler, *Joshua*, Word Biblical Commentary (Waco: Word, 1983), 216.

[3] Walter C. Kaiser, Jr., *Toward Old Testament Ethics* (Grand Rapids: Zondervan, 1983), 165-68.

high priest has died' (Num. 35:32). Hence Gordon J. Wenham infers:

> Both incur blood guilt and pollute the land, and both require atonement: murder by the execution of the murderer and manslaughter through the natural demise of the high priest.[4]

Not all interpreters accept this inference, but the passage does seem to teach that the high priest's death is the only ransom for the manslayer, that his death, in some way, atones for the blood shed and satisfies the claims of justice. Only the high priest's death can release the offender from his banishment and bring him home again: a remarkable picture of what our 'merciful and faithful high priest' (Heb. 2:17) has done for us.

The Circle of Yahweh's Justice
Finally, we must note how the circle of Yahweh's justice includes the sojourner as well as the native Israelite: 'These are the cities appointed for all the sons of Israel and for the sojourner who sojourns among them...' (v. 9). Verse 9 is a summary note for the chapter; yet it is a typical summary of Yahweh's character, the God who includes the sojourner (Hebrew, *ger*) within his justice because he has included him within his love (Deut. 10:18).[5] There *is* a wideness in God's mercy. Here, already in Joshua, we meet the God who will delight to 'bring near those who are far off by the blood of the Messiah' (Eph. 2:13). Even summary statements reveal God's character and call us to fall down and worship our just and compassionate God.

---

[4] Gordon J. Wenham, *Numbers*, Tyndale Old Testament Commentaries (Leicester: Inter-Varsity, 1981), 238; also Gustav Friedrich Oehler, *Theology of the Old Testament*, 8th ed. (New York and London: Funk and Wagnalls, 1883), 237-38; and C. F. Keil and Franz Delitzsch, *The Pentateuch,* Biblical Commentary on the Old Testament (1868; reprint ed.; Grand Rapids: Eerdmans, n.d.), 3:264-66.

[5] A *ger* was 'a permanent resident, once a citizen of another land, who had moved into his new residence', often leaving his homeland under some distress; Merrill F. Unger and William White, Jr., eds., *Nelson's Expository Dictionary of the Old Testament* (Nashville: Thomas Nelson, 1980), 387. For an excellent summary on the *ger* (pronounced gay-er), see L. L. Walker, 'Sojourner', *ZPEB*, 5:468-69.

Yahweh's Sojourners (21:1-42)

Secondly, the allotting of the levitical cities in 21:1-42 gives a glimpse of Yahweh's sojourners. The tribe of Levi was not to receive a given inheritance like other tribes (13:14, 33); rather the Levites were to reside in certain cities specified for them throughout Israel (14:3-4).[6]

The structure of 21:1-42 is clear and easy to trace. Broadly, it is:

1. Levitical cities claimed in faith, verses 1-3
2. Levitical cities determined by lot, verses 4-8
3. Levitical cities listed by name, verses 9-40

In both the lot summary (vv. 4-8) and the name list (vv. 9-40) we meet an orderly sequence: Kohathites who are Aaron's descendants (thirteen cities), the rest of the Kohathites (ten cities), the Gershonites (thirteen cities), and the Merarites (twelve cities).

The Authority They Claim

Observe the authority the Levites claim in verses 1-3. Yahweh had instructed Moses that Israel was to give the Levites cities where they could live and pasturage around those cities for their livestock (Num. 35:1-8). The Levites had not forgotten. They approached Eleazar, Joshua, and the Israelite leadership to ask that they now be given what Yahweh had authorised for them. Already Caleb (14:6ff.) and the daughters of Zelophedad (17:3-6) had followed this pattern. Both near the beginning and at the close of this third major section of Joshua (chs. 13–21) we have people (Caleb and the Levites, respectively) coming to claim what Yahweh had promised them.

It is not too extreme to say that this should be the normal pattern for all believing prayer, namely, that we seek what 'Yahweh commanded ... to give us' (v. 2). What God has promised us, what God has authorised us to have, we should seek in prayer. We usually give too little thought to what God actually has promised us. Perhaps we too frequently and

---

[6] Obviously, the Levites weren't the only residents of such towns; they lived among the other Israelites there (cf. 21:11-12).

glibly think that 'every promise in the Book is mine', when, actually, it isn't. That is why, in John Calvin's view, the Lord's Prayer is so valuable:

> For [God] prescribed a form for us in which he set forth as in a table all that he allows us to seek of him, all that is of benefit to us, all that we need ask. From this kindness of his we receive great fruit of consolation: that we know we are requesting nothing absurd, nothing strange or unseemly – in short, nothing unacceptable to him – since we are asking almost in his own words.[7]

Or take James 1:5 in context. There we are assured that if we lack wisdom to know how to respond to and act in our trials (vv. 2-4), we should ask God for it in faith, and the giving God will give it to us. Such a promise can be restated and turned into a prayer.

What confidence then we should have as we ask for God's rule to come on earth. What assurance of being heard when we ask for provision of our food, pardon for our sins, and protection from our tempter. Perhaps even the Levites and their cities can teach us to pray.

The Provision They Need

When the Levites request their cities they are asking only for the provision they need. Certainly the priests and Levites were set apart for a special ministry in Israel, for example, offering sacrifice and caring for and maintaining the tabernacle (see Num. 3–4).[8] But though one might say they performed spiritual functions, they had very earthly needs – houses to live in, pastures to sustain livestock.[9]

There is a given earthiness about all of life. That is no less true for those sometimes dubbed, in a quasi-technical sense, God's servants. God's people must keep this in mind. I know,

---

[7] John Calvin, *Institutes of the Christian Religion*, ed. John T. McNeill, trans. Ford Lewis Battles, 2 vols. (Philadelphia: Westminster, 1960), 3.20.34.

[8] For detailed treatment see David A. Hubbard, 'Priests and Levites', *IDB*, 2:1266-73.

[9] Karl Gutbrod (*Das buch vom Lande Gottes*, Die Botschaft des Alten Testaments, 3d ed. [Stuttgart: Calwer, 1965], 133) nicely touches on this point.

of course, that there are pastors, evangelists, and various Christian workers who are in their ministries for fun and profit, primarily profit; and that there are some who are not apparently driven by mammon but who are poor stewards and undiscerning spenders and therefore always 'need' more. Sometimes, however, it is God's people who are strangely (or conveniently) oblivious to the physical needs of those who serve them. A church may pay its pastor a scraping wage and forget that he, too, is a human who needs medical insurance, a retirement fund, and some way to educate his children (not to mention that they may need new tennis shoes this year). Or a church supports a Christian staff worker on a college campus. There's only the staff worker and his young wife and man does not live by bread alone. So we gladly let him feed on the Scriptures but not on sandwiches or spaghetti or – certainly not! – steak. In some quarters there is still the idea that a missionary would never need to buy new clothes (whom do you think the mission barrel at the church is for?) or purchase make-up (is it right for female missionaries to be attractive?). The priests and Levites have not carried us on a tangent. What is implicit in Joshua 21 is clearly taught by the apostle in 1 Corinthians 9.

The Parable They Live

Again, the Levites remind us of the parable they live. Since the Levites received no land as inheritance but only cities to live in (see, again, 13:14, 33; 14:3-4), they really have the status of sojourners.[10] Indeed, Deuteronomy 18:6 uses this word (sojourns) to describe the Levites' residence in one of Israel's towns. In one sense, since they never owned land, they would not develop roots. Some people saw that the Levites' life was really a parable for every Israelite's life and sensed that there is a certain rootlessness to every man's existence – even that of the people of God. For example, David prayed: 'For we are sojourners before Thee, and tenants, as all our fathers were; our days on the earth are like a shadow, and there is no hope' (1 Chron. 29:15, NASB). In Psalm 39:12 he pleads that God

---

[10] See my remarks on 20:9 on the sojourner.

would hear his prayer, 'for I am a sojourner with you, a settler like all my fathers'. So the Levite is a parable for us to see and hear, a sort of visual aid of our fleeting, transitory, rootless existence. A reminder that we must always say, 'If the Lord wills, we live and do this or that' (James 4:15), a nudge that 'even we ourselves who have the firstfruits, namely the Spirit, go on groaning within ourselves as we expect the adoption, that is, the redemption of our body' (Rom. 8:23). Yet, strangely, recognising this Levite aspect of our lives does not bring us to despair but to reality; it nurtures a certain humility that in turn begets hope in the Living One, who has the keys of Death and Hades (Rev. 1:17-18).

The Calling They Have

Before leaving the Levites and their cities, we might consider the calling they have. Just why is it that they are to be scattered in these cities all over Israel? This passage does not answer this question. But Calvin may well have been reading Providence correctly when he holds that they were appointed

> as a kind of guardians in every district to retain the people in the pure worship of God. It is true, they were everywhere strangers; but still it was with the very high dignity of acting as stewards for God, and preventing their countrymen from revolting from piety. This is the reason for stating so carefully how many cities they obtained from each tribe; they were everywhere to keep watch, and preserve the purity of sacred rites unimpaired.[11]

Calvin's view is more than a sharp guess. The tribe of Levi was to furnish not only the priests for the altar but also teachers for the law (Deut. 33:10) and, at various times, we see Levites or priests doing just that (2 Chron. 17:7-9; 35:3; Neh. 8:7-9; see also Mal. 2:4-7). Hence, the 'purpose of the allotment of these cities was surely related to the special Levitical ministry of covenant teaching among the twelve tribes'. The levitical cities were meant to serve as 'bases of operation so that the Levites could better infiltrate each of the tribes to instruct them in Yahweh's covenant'.[12]

---

[11] John Calvin, *Commentaries on the Book of Joshua*, trans. Henry Beveridge, in vol. 4 of *Calvin's Commentaries*, 22 vols. (reprint ed.; Grand Rapids: Baker, 1981), 246.

[12] G. P. Hugenberger, 'Levitical Cities', *ISBE*, rev. ed., 3:109.

The New Testament church knew the same urgency of 'teaching every man in all wisdom' (Col. 1:28). Paul directs Timothy: 'What you have heard from me through many witnesses entrust to faithful men, who will also be qualified to teach others' (2 Tim. 2:2). The church usually stands in need of a beneficent Levite conspiracy to instruct the people of God in leading a godly life and in developing a covenant mind. Some Christians acutely sense the need for this. They tell you that their church preaches the call of the gospel but does not teach the depth of the gospel. There are churches that love to count but not to feed the sheep.

The mention of Jattir, Eshtemoa, or Holon (vv. 14-15) may not send chills of excitement up the spine of today's Christian, but the Levites and their cities have more to say to him than he may realise.

Yahweh's Fidelity (21:43-45)

Lastly, we must look at the grand testimony of Yahweh's fidelity. This passage is the theological heart of the Book of Joshua; it deliberately echoes the concerns of 1:1-9 (cf. especially 1:2-3, 5-6) and structurally draws a line across everything that has preceded. Here is the jugular vein of the book. Yet two major commentaries published within the last twenty years allot nine and five lines respectively to this section: an inexcusable blunder.

Karl Gutbrod has noted that verse 43 (the land where Israel lives) aptly summarises chapters 13–21, while verse 44 (the conflicts with Israel's enemies) summarises the victories of chapters 1–12, with verse 45 encompassing the whole narrative of Joshua.[13] It seems our writer has deliberately and thoughtfully placed these verses at just this point.

Certainly, some find problems here. These statements seem so final and conclusive, and some worry about the other considerations, namely, that there remained much land to be possessed (13:1) and there were enemies that Israel was not driving out (e.g. 16:10; 17:12-13). But we must remember that the biblical writer (or, if someone prefers, final editor) knew of these other factors, and, if he had thought them to be directly

---

[13] Gutbrod, *Das Buch vom Lande Gottes*, 137.

contradictory to 21:43-45, he would surely have noticed it (and, presumably, addressed the matter). Apparently the biblical writer felt no unbearable rub here. (Too often biblical criticism fails to realise that the biblical writers had at least as much sense as we do and could certainly observe contradictions and inconsistencies when they saw them.) Yahweh had given Israel all the land (v. 43a) – witness the fact that they possessed and lived in it (v. 43b). The fact that they might possess still more of it (cf. Exod. 23:30) does not negate this. Moreover, our previous comments on 13:1 pointed out how substantial Israelite dominance really was in the land, according to the biblical text. And Yahweh had given rest to Israel (v. 44a; see also 22:4) – witness the record of their victories (v. 44b; see chs. 1–12). If there are more battles to fight and offensives to launch, these do not negate the rest Yahweh has given to date.

PRAISE TO YAHWEH

However, if one must choose, it is far better to hear the word than to explain its difficulties. There is no doubt about what we hear at this point. One can only describe 21:43-45 as praise – praise to Yahweh for complete, thorough, persistent fidelity to his promises. Remember that verses 43-45 gather up all of Joshua so far. In this they function like Romans 11:33-36 in relation to Paul's preceding chapters. In view of the massive, mysterious, insistent mercies of God, the apostle throws up his hands: 'O how deep the wealth of God's wisdom and knowledge!' (Rom. 11:33a). So at Joshua 21:43-45: O how firm the word and promise of God!

The writer uses what I would call sledgehammer theology; he simply keeps pounding his point home. By emphatic repetition he pummels Yahweh's fidelity into our senses. Note the references to 'what he had sworn' (v. 43), 'according to all that he had sworn' (v. 44), 'the good promise that Yahweh had spoken' (v. 45). In every case Yahweh gave what he swore, not a word fell, everything came about. There were no falling words!

So these are theological statements, but statements that worship, statements that praise Yahweh. Theology is always at its best when it includes doxology, when it cannot speak without at the same time worshipping. However, Yahweh's fidelity (and hence the reason for praising him) appears all the brighter when viewed in the light of preceding salvation history. For the promise of the land given to Abraham (Gen. 12:7; 13:14-17; 15:7, for example) never did look like it had a chance of fulfilment (this is the real point of Genesis 12:6b). Indeed, the only land Abraham ever received was Sarah's cemetery (Gen. 23), and he had to buy that. Abraham had his own struggles with Yahweh's promise of land (Gen. 15:8-16). Then Yahweh tells him, 'Your descendants will be exiles in a land not their own, where they will be slaves and oppressed for four hundred years' (Gen. 15:13, JB). So not only did Abraham himself not receive 'what was promised' (Heb. 11:39), but its fulfilment was put off for an extended time – and time has its own way of withering faith in God's promises.

Surely a promise made so long ago must have expired. And now they must endure bondage (Exod. 1–15). These slaves of Pharaoh hardly looked like heirs of Yahweh. Surely they would die making Egypt's bricks rather than live eating Canaan's figs. But in the fullness of time God sent forth his plagues into Pharaoh's heart until he relented and, unbelievably, God led his people toward his land. Then, as if time and slavery were not enough, it seemed that God's own people had conspired to frustrate his promise (Num. 13–14). Forty years were then spent wandering in the wilderness.

Only when we see the barriers Yahweh smashes in order to fulfil his word, only when we see his promise trampling all apparent obstacles put in its way, only then will we appreciate how tenacious our God's fidelity is to his promise and his people.

My father was a pastor. Once when I was a teenager my mother told me that my father had hurried home from pastoral calling one afternoon because he thought he had promised me that I could use the family car. As a matter of fact, he hadn't. But I got a glimpse of his character from that: nothing was going to prevent him from keeping a promise to his son, even if it only involved using the car. That is the unstoppability we see in Yahweh's faithfulness to his word. Therefore, the order of the day is worship.

A Promise for Us

Besides expressing praise, this section also contains a promise for us. In verse 44 it is clear that the rest God gave Israel consisted primarily in victory over their enemies: 'not a man of all their enemies stood before them; all their enemies Yahweh gave into their hand'. 'The rest obtained for Israel had as its necessary corollary the defeat of Israel's *enemies*'[14] (see Exod. 23:22). This is always the case; there is no rest or peace unless the opposition to God and his people is removed. The pattern is the same in the New Testament, for the apostle comforts believers suffering persecution by promising that God

> will pay back trouble to those who trouble you and give relief [or, rest] to you who are troubled, and to us as well. This will happen when the Lord Jesus is revealed from heaven in blazing fire with his powerful angels. He will punish those who do not know God and do not obey the gospel of our Lord Jesus. They will be punished with everlasting destruction and shut out from the presence of the Lord and from the majesty of his power... [2 Thess. 1:6-9, NIV].

This may appear harsh. It is. But the only way lasting rest can be given to God's people is by the decisive cutting off of their enemies. Otherwise they are never secure.

We too easily and sentimentally forget all this. When we pray, 'Thy kingdom come, thy will be done, *on earth* as it is in heaven', we surely don't suppose this will come as a result of a unanimous United Nations' resolution with which all nations immediately and gladly comply (rather, see Ps. 2). Such rest and peace will lastingly come only when Christ visibly conquers all his and our enemies. This is the promise of Joshua 21. Yahweh gave Israel rest when he defeated their enemies. This is the biblical pattern. It serves, then, as a foreshadowing of Jesus' victory (see again 2 Thess. 1:7-10) and our rest. When King Jesus delivers us from the evil one and his allies, then there will be no more terror in the night nor arrow flying by day, and a saint will be perfectly safe sitting under his vine or fig tree (Mic. 4:4).

---

[14] Marten H. Woudstra, *The Book of Joshua*, The New International Commentary on the Old Testament (Grand Rapids: Eerdmans, 1981), 315.

STUDY QUESTIONS:

1. How do the cities of refuge help us to understand God's idea of justice?

2. Why do you think that the cities of refuge were both a refuge and a prison?

3. Do you agree with the proposition that the death of the High Priest is a type of ransom for the manslayer or is it merely a picture of enough time served?

4. Why was God so concerned to include the sojourner in his conditions for the cities of refuge?

5. Does Yahweh's fidelity to you cause you to worship him or do you simply expect his fidelity?

Part 4

Retaining the Land

(Joshua 22–24)

19

What Can an Altar Alter?
(Joshua 22)

We have just entered the last major division of the Book of Joshua. The whole breaks down like this:

Entering the land, chapters 1–4
Taking the land, chapters 5–12
Possessing the land, chapters 13–21
Retaining the land, chapters 22–24

We should note the function of chapters 22–24 before we focus on chapter 22 by itself. Observe that each of these last three chapters begins when Joshua summons (Hebrew, *qara'*) Israel or some significant segment of it (22:1; 23:2; 24:1). Thus the book closes with three assemblies of the people of God. Remember that all this immediately follows the heavy theological text, 21:43-45, which emphatically underscores Yahweh's fidelity to his promise. By contrast, chapters 22–24 are preoccupied with the theme of Israel's fidelity to Yahweh (22:5, 16, 18, 19, 25, 29, 31; 23:6, 8, 11; 24:14-15, 16, 18, 21, 23, 24).[1] Hence the last three chapters constitute the writer's major application: Israel must respond in kind to Yahweh's unwavering faithfulness. Willing

---

[1] Yet even within these chapters, Israel's fidelity is consistently based on Yahweh's antecedent fidelity (e.g. 23:5, 9-10, 14; 24:2-13, 17-18).

bondage to this faithful God is their only rational and proper response. The logic is that of the 'therefore' of Romans 12:1 as it follows the divine mercies of Romans 1–11. In principle it is the same as 'love so amazing, so divine, demands my soul, my life, my all'.

These last three chapters pose the question: Whither Israel? Our writer spends three chapters charting the right course for them. How crucial Israel's answer to Yahweh will be! It will determine whether Israel retains the land (23:12-13, 15-16; 24:20). The writer or editor may see a small cloud rising that bodes ill (24:31).

A comment is appropriate here about the possible life-setting of the Book of Joshua or about the particular audience it may have addressed. I suggest that Joshua, substantially as it stands,[2] would prove potent preaching material to the Judges generation (Judg. 2:6-10) who were slack about driving out the remnants of the Canaanites (Judg. 1:27–2:5; cf. Josh. 16:10; 17:12-18; 18:3), and therefore created a climate for apostasy to occur in a most predictable way (Judg. 2:11–3:6; cf. Josh. 23:6-7, 11-13).[3] A faithful disciple of Yahweh seeing the sophomore generation slowly losing its vision of its gracious God and sliding toward apostasy wants Israel to know the work Yahweh had done for them (Judg. 2:10). Hence, he rehearses the power and fidelity of Yahweh in the original conquest story (chs. 1–12) and even wraps the archives in exhortation and admonition (14:6-15; 17:14-18; 18:3). Then in a threefold application he drives home that Israel should and must always be slaves of Yahweh (chs. 22–24). Not that the book wouldn't speak to still later generations and situations; but one need look no further than thirty or forty years after Joshua's death for a most appropriate audience urgently needing the kerygma of Joshua.[4]

---

[2] I am not averse to the concept of some later editing.

[3] Many biblical critics would question using Judges 2:11–3:6 as accurate historical material since they see there a later Deuteronomic hand editing. But the Deuteronomic hand in Judges 2–3 is more scholarly shibboleth than reality. Milking the details of the text shows rather little proven D influence. I have spelled this out in tedious and dull detail in 'A Proposed Life-Setting for the Book of Judges' (University Microfilms, 1978), 137-42, 157-69.

[4] A number of biblical critics would smile at such a naïve proposal. To take the Book of Joshua as a unified entity at such an early date stretches credulity to

Now to chapter 22; let us try to mount the right hermeneutical horse at the outset. Clearly, the keynote of this chapter is the pervasive passion for fidelity to Yahweh (e.g. vv. 5, 19, 29, 31). Hence, we must beware of moralising the text into anything less, such as the peril of rumour, the tragedy of misunderstanding, or the need to talk out problems reasonably. Those may be commendable concerns, but they do not constitute the main freight of chapter 22.

A Gracious Commendation (22:1-8)
We find here a gracious commendation of the two-and-a-half eastern tribes on the part of Joshua (vv. 1-8). Joshua's commendation for obedience (vv. 1-4) precedes an exhortation to fidelity (v. 5) and a direction regarding generosity (vv. 6, 7b-8).

This passage picks up 1:12-18. There Joshua had charged the Reubenites, Gadites, and half of Manasseh who had settled east of the Jordan to send their fighting men over into Canaan and to assist their brothers (1:14-15) in conquering

---

say nothing of credibility. For them the hypothesis is too simple and too early. But evidence is not lacking for an early date; see R. K. Harrison, *Introduction to the Old Testament* (Grand Rapids: Eerdmans, 1969), 666-73; Kenneth A. Kitchen, 'The Old Testament in Its Context: 3 from Joshua to Solomon', *TSF Bulletin* 61 (Autumn 1971): 6-7 (my life-setting suggestion reflects Kitchen's); and B. K. Waltke, 'Joshua, Book of', *ISBE*, rev. ed., 2:1134-38. Simplicity is, in my book, a plus; the more complicated an explanatory critical theory becomes, the less probability it holds of being correct, since every additional element inserts new (frequently uncheckable) variables into the problem. Multiplying the variables in a theory multiplies the uncertainty of their (all) describing the true course of events. Whether for a book or a chapter, the customary critical proposals inspire less confidence than a naïve one. For chapter 22, someone will hold we have a Gilgal tradition and a Shiloh tradition – these may have been in conflict originally. Of course, a Deuteronomic editor contributes his material, and a Priestly hand adds his touches – nor must we forget another post-exilic redactor (cf. the commentaries by Gray and Soggin on Joshua 22). Someone else will speculate differently. There are no controls; it is sheer guesswork. What's more, it seldom makes any difference (except to place question marks after the reliability of Scripture).

The real problem with such bloodless speculation is that, after having done it, its practitioners strangely enough do not bother to tell us what their literary monstrosity has to say to the flock of God. The problem with most commentaries of such genre is that they can in no way nourish the church in godliness. Do they provide technical help – linguistic, archaeological? Yes. But to them the Scripture is not warm. It is an artifact from the past, not an oracle from God. Nor should they wonder if the church finds all their furrow-browed, pin-the-tail-on-the-tradition-centre activity next to useless.

their territory. They had complied and are now commended: 'You have kept all that Moses commanded you' (v. 2); 'you listened to my voice' (v. 2); 'you have not forsaken your brothers' (v. 3).

How beautiful such obedience is! It should remind all of God's people that obedience really is a live option. It is possible not to sin (1 John 2:1). No one knows the virility of sin like the saints of God, and sometimes in our struggle with sin we can wearily come to think that we are doomed to lose the fight. We need the right perspective: sin will *not* lord it over us, for we are under the sway of King Grace (Rom. 6:14).

There is also something significant in the fact that Joshua can commend these tribes. There is much to commend the practice of commending God's people when it may be done sincerely. In fact, it is quite commendable! As Matthew Henry observed:

> Though it was by the favour of God and his power that Israel got possession of this land, and he must have all the glory, yet Joshua thought there was a thankful acknowledgment due to their brethren who assisted them, and whose sword and bow were employed for them. God must be chiefly eyed in our praises, yet instruments must not be altogether overlooked.[5]

Pastors and other Christian workers should heed such counsel. We can be a rather negative lot, always able to see where most of the holes in the kirk dike are, knowing who the most obstreperous saints are, and aware of how many uncleansed spots and unpressed wrinkles remain in the church's robe. But there is the elder who thoughtfully leads the congregation in worship or who conscientiously checks on the welfare of the flock; there is the school teacher who holds a steadfast witness among her peers and her students; there is the couple that calls on other believers in distress. One is sometimes surprised how such servants find encouragement and gain fresh heart from a pastor or friend expressing gratitude for their labour done in love.

The burden of Joshua's words comes in verse 5 in his emphatic exhortation to faithfulness:

---

[5] Matthew Henry, *Commentary on the Whole Bible*, 6 vols. (New York: Revell, n.d.), 2:102.

Only be very careful to do the commandment and the torah which Moses the servant of Yahweh commanded you, to love Yahweh your God and to walk in all his ways, and to keep his commandments and to cling to him and to serve him with all your heart and with all your being.[6]

The context is instructive: he commends before he commands. He is not being utilitarian or manipulative. It is rather a biblical pattern. Paul will spend three chapters in expressing thanksgiving and joy over the Thessalonians before he begins to command and instruct them (1 Thess. 1–3, then 4–5). The risen Lord tends to commend before he critiques in Revelation 2–3 ('I know … I have this against you'). So long as it is done in accord with truth, one should always prefer to win than to force the obedience of the saints, to encourage fidelity rather than exact it.

A Vigilant Fidelity (22:9-20)

Secondly, we see what a vigilant fidelity the western tribes display (vv. 9-20). The eastern tribes depart from Shiloh (v. 9) and build a giant altar;[7] the western tribes hear of the altar and assemble at Shiloh (v. 12). These then send a delegation under the direction of Phinehas to inquire into the matter (vv. 13-15) before they actually engage in war (v. 12). In verses 16-20 they express their concern (i.e. alarm) to the eastern tribes. But why all the fuss over building an altar? How could they be rebelling against Yahweh? What could an altar alter?

A look at Deuteronomy 12 answers this.[8] There Israel is commanded to offer their only sacrifices only at 'the place that Yahweh your God will choose' out of all Israel's tribes (Deut. 12:5, 13-14). This 'place' stands opposed to 'all the places' where the Canaanites had customarily conducted their orgies

---

[6] The Hebrew root *shamar* (to keep, to guard, to be careful to do something) appears five times in verses 2-5 (vv. 2, 3 [twice], 5 [twice], but a uniform English translation is difficult.

[7] I think the altar was on the west side of the Jordan, but others view verses 10-11 differently. One can check the commentaries if interested.

[8] A warm debate simmers over just what Deuteronomy 12 does require. For the passage itself, cf. P. C. Craigie, *The Book of Deuteronomy*, The New International Commentary on the Old Testament (Grand Rapids: Eerdmans, 1976), 216-18. For perspective on the whole critical debate, see Gordon J. Wenham, 'Deuteronomy and the Central Sanctuary', *Tyndale Bulletin* 22 (1971): 103-18.

(Deut. 12:2-3). The restriction of sacrifice to one sanctuary was preventive theology, intended to preserve the purity of worship. To oversimplify, it meant: one altar, one faith, one people. But allow such worship wherever folks hankered to 'experience God', and it would soon take on a Canaanite color, soak up Canaanite belief, sport Canaanite practices, adore Canaanite gods. In short, it would at one blow kill both fidelity to Yahweh and the unity of Israel. So to the western tribes wind of another altar suggested man-chosen worship and sacrifice and reeked of the first step toward apostasy.

Some do not understand the potential peril here and so score the western tribes, bemoaning the tragedy of misunderstanding:

> There is something ugly about human nature. The moment disagreements arise, the immediate reaction is a resort to arms. The Israelites made no attempt to understand. At once there was a determination to fight it out and to eliminate those whom they had misjudged. Without attempting to find the truth, they rushed 'to make war' [this hardly squares with vv. 13-14]. There is not much of sweet reasonableness in the world. The problem of all time is how to put the round table of common negotiation in place of arbitrament of the sword.[9]

There is a tragedy of misunderstanding here, but it is the expositor's and not Israel's. It is rather a sign of health that Israel is so stirred by even the appearance of unfaithfulness.

The western tribes stress that any infidelity by the two-and-a-half tribes would place all Israel under Yahweh's anger. The

---

[9] Joseph R. Sizoo, 'The Book of Joshua: Exposition', *The Interpreter's Bible*, 12 vols. (New York: Abingdon, 1953), 2:658. George Bush drew a wholly different (and I would hold, correct) estimate of the western tribes: 'Their holy jealousy, therefore, in these circumstances was no more than a proper expression of their intense concern for the glory of God and the honor of his institutions. But their zeal was tempered with the meekness of wisdom, and before proceeding to extremities they determined to send an embassy to inquire into facts, and if their suspicions were confirmed, to see whether they could not be prevailed upon by milder methods to abandon their wicked enterprise.... Instead of saying that the case was too clear to admit of doubt, or too gross to allow of apology, they evidently go on the presumption that they *may* have been mistaken in their construction of the affair, and that at any rate it was proper that they should not condemn their brethren unheard, but should give them the opportunity of justifying themselves in the measure if it were possible' (*Notes, Critical and Practical, on the Book of Joshua* [Chicago: Henry A. Sumner, 1881], 193-94).

Baal Peor fiasco (Num. 25) brought Yahweh's plague against the congregation (v. 17), and they were still wallowing in some of Peor's mire. If the eastern tribes rebel today, Yahweh's wrath will strike 'all the congregation of Israel' tomorrow (v. 18). If they rebel, it will 'cause us to rebel' (repointing the Hebrew verb in v. 19; cf. RSV). Remember Achan (v. 20; see ch. 7)! That was only one man's act – but he didn't suffer alone. One man's act of treachery[10] placed the whole congregation under divine wrath.

Small wonder the western tribes are aroused. They know that sin permitted brings judgment on all, that unfaithfulness tolerated will infect still more.

> Here, then, we have an illustrious display of piety, teaching us that if we see the pure worship of God corrupted, we must be strenuous, to the utmost of our ability, in vindicating it.[11]

How the church needs to recover such a passionate piety, such an infatuation for the true worship of God, such an anxiety when covenant people appear to wander from the path. The church then should hold members under vigilant (I did not say vicious) discipline. Part of the problem in our day is that many erroneously assume that the church is a democracy; that, therefore, pluralism (even in essential doctrines) is to be expected, allowed, and welcomed, for, after all, who are we to judge others or bring them under discipline? We must be nice to people, you know, or they will leave the church. But the church is not a democracy; rather, she lives under the kingship of Jesus, who has entrusted the care of his flock to elders, who are to guard, protect, and discipline it (Acts 20:28; 1 Pet. 5:1-4). Certainly the undershepherds of Christ's flock must apply New Testament principles of discipline in the church – but they will find the proper attitude toward their task in Joshua 22.

---

[10] The root *m' l* (treachery, to commit treachery) and the verb *marad* (to revolt, rebel) both appear four times in verses 16-20.

[11] John Calvin, *Commentaries on the Book of Joshua,* trans. Henry Beveridge, in vol. 4 of *Calvin's Commentaries,* 22 vols. (reprint ed.; Grand Rapids: Baker 1981), 254.

A Godly Anxiety (22:21-29)

A third observation is that the Transjordan tribes have a godly anxiety for the pure worship of God (vv. 21-29). What a happy irony: Israel fears the altar is an expression of infidelity (vv. 13-20), while the eastern tribes affirm it is a means of preventing infidelity.

The eastern tribes go on oath that they had no unfaithful intention in their altar-building episode; let both Yahweh and Israel take vengeance if they did (vv. 21-23). Instead, their altar was the fruit of their anxiety (Hebrew, *de' agah*, v. 24) for the future (*machar*, literally, 'tomorrow', in vv. 24, 27, 28). They were afraid that in a generation or so the descendants of the western tribes would treat their descendants with disdain, view the Jordan River as a Berlin Wall, and consider the eastern tribes as no part of Yahweh's people. After all, the westerners could say, the eastern tribes weren't settled in the real land of promise.[12] If they don't live in Yahweh's land, how can they claim to be Yahweh's people? So it would go. The upshot would be that 'your sons might make our sons stop fearing Yahweh' (v. 25).

There was good reason for such anxiety. They had rightly named the Jordan River as the potential geographical culprit behind such division. It is difficult for us, living in a bridge culture, to appreciate what a barrier to communication the Jordan Valley posed. In the nineteenth century George Adam Smith described it this way:

> There may be something on the surface of another planet to match the Jordan Valley: there is nothing on this. No other part of our earth, uncovered by water, sinks to 300 feet below the level of the ocean. But here we have a rift more than one hundred and sixty miles long, and from two to fifteen broad, which falls from the sea-level to as deep as 1292 feet below it at the coast of the Dead Sea, while the bottom of the latter is 1300 feet deeper still. In this trench there are the Jordan, a river nearly one hundred miles long; two great lakes, respectively twelve and fifty-three miles in length.[13]

---

[12] See Numbers 32 and Gordon J. Wenham, *Numbers*, Tyndale Old Testament Commentaries (Leicester: Inter-Varsity, 1981), 212-13.

[13] George Adam Smith, *The Historical Geography of the Holy Land*, 22d ed. (London: Hodder and Stoughton, n.d.), 468-69. See also D. Baly, *The Geography*

'This colossal ditch' was Smith's term for the Jordan Valley. One wishes the two-and-a-half tribes would have had the foresight to think of this difficulty in Numbers 32 rather than in Joshua 22.

Nevertheless, at least here they are concerned. Here they are 'anxious about tomorrow' (cf. Matt. 6:34) in a way even Jesus, I think, would commend. In fact, our Lord would probably instruct us: 'Worry then like this' (à la Matt. 6:9). For here is worthy worry and proper anxiety: to care about whether one's seed will be faithful to God and to take all necessary measures to insure that it might be so. Let Israel again teach us to communicate the faith to our children in diligent, interesting, persistent teaching; to pray for them and with them; to pray even for grandchildren and great-grandchildren not yet born, that Yahweh will grant us a 'godly seed' (cf. Mal. 2:15). There is nothing quaint in George Bush's lament:

> Yet, alas! how much more anxious are thousands to entail upon their descendants ample worldly possessions, even at the hazard of all their better interests, than to perpetuate among them those invaluable means of grace which take hold on eternal life! God forbid that we should ever be willing that our children should dwell in splendid mansions, or revel in accumulated riches, on which 'Ichabod' is written![14]

At least the Transjordan tribes could provide against one future pitfall. If Israel should ever suggest that the easterners had 'no portion in Yahweh', the latter could point to the altar their ancestors had erected just after the conquest. A strange altar indeed! Not for burnt-offering or sacrifice but for witness – a perpetual witness that Yahweh belonged to the residents of Gilead no less than to those of Canaan.

West and East leave us with a paradox that, if swallowed whole, will give us the right balance. The western tribes argued that unity cannot exist with apostasy (vv. 13-20), while the eastern tribes feared that fidelity cannot exist without unity (vv. 21-29). This eastern emphasis stands behind

---

of the Bible (New York: Harper and Brothers, 1957), 218. Neither Reuben nor Gad seems to have come to Israel's aid in the Jabin-Sisera episode (Judg. 5:15b-17a). Was the Jordan the wall?

[14] Bush, *Joshuai, 198.*

Hebrews 10:24-25 and is part of the reason Paul seared Peter
and friends for ceasing table fellowship with gentile Christians
(Gal. 2:11-21).

A Satisfying Resolution (22:30-34)

Finally, the whole matter comes to a satisfying resolution
(vv. 30-34). Everyone seems pleased and relieved.

Phinehas speaks for the tribal committee: 'Today we know
that Yahweh is among us because you have delivered the sons
of Israel from Yahweh's hand' (v. 31). The sign of Yahweh's
presence is that his people have been kept from falling and
so have been kept from his judgment ('Yahweh's hand').
Phinehas both commends the Gilead tribes and praises
Yahweh; in essence he says that we know God's presence
when he protects us from his own judgment. That is exactly
what happened at the cross and what is behind the doctrine
of propitiation.[15] How much more clearly can we know God is
for us than when he shields us from his own wrath by placing
us under the shelter of his Son's cross?

The sons of Israel are satisfied (v. 33). In fact, they bless
God, evidently because their attack-and-destroy mission
was no longer necessary (v. 33b). Hence they praise God for
causing his peace to rule among his people (cf. Col. 3:15).

The eastern tribes reaffirm the intention behind their altar:
'it is a witness between us that Yahweh is God' (v. 34b). In
Old Testament faith there is no more crucial confession than
'Yahweh is God' (see Deut. 4:32-40, especially vv. 35, 39, and
1 Kings 18:21, 24, 36, 37, 39), just as 'Jesus is Lord' (1 Cor. 12:3)
stands at the centre of the New Testament faith. From the
flow of the story we know that they mean to say, 'Yahweh is
our God as well as yours, and therefore we are one people.'
Joshua 22 declares that it is truth that unifies the people of
God; apart from truth there can be no unity. So God's people
here declare their witness to his truth.

Would that all the conflicts among God's people would
end with such clear evidence of his presence, his peace, and
his truth!

---

[15] Which is, as J. I. Packer puts it, 'the heart of the gospel'; see *Knowing God*
(Downers Grove: Inter-Varsity, 1973), 161-80.

STUDY QUESTIONS:

1. Do you believe that there is enough gracious commendation of one another in the church today?

2. Is there a fear to exercise church discipline against believers in our churches today? Why or why not?

3. Why does style of worship seem to be more important that content of worship? Does it really matter?

4. Have you ever had a godly anxiety for things that you have seen happening in the church?

5. When there is unity in the body of Christ is there thanksgiving to God or just 'slaps on the backs' of one another? In other words, when there is unity, who gets the glory?

20

Staying on Edge
(Joshua 23)

When you drive in a heavy downpour or a thick fog you psych yourself up to an extra measure of alertness. Your eyes try to peer fifteen feet farther than is possible to see; your body tenses in order to act should any sudden development require it. It's all very tiring, and you long for a return to more normal conditions so you can relax. It's tough to stay on edge for very long. Yet even under normal conditions both highway and town driving require quite a degree of alertness – not necessarily edginess but of staying on edge.

That is Joshua's concern in chapter 23. It is one thing for Israel to stay up for (perhaps) a five-year conquest; it is another to maintain the vigour and vision over the long haul in order to complete the conquest and preserve its results.

Here, then, is the second of the three assemblies with which the Book of Joshua closes (see discussion on ch. 22). The emphasis remains on the necessity for fidelity to Yahweh (vv. 6, 8, 11) in order to retain the land (vv. 13, 15, 16). Here an aged Joshua addresses Israel through her leaders in his last will and testament.

Sometimes it is useful to sketch the structure or development of a section of text in order to see in short compass where it is going. In chapter 23 Joshua sets forth an argument for continuing fidelity to Yahweh, which unfolds like this:

Anticipation of Yahweh's help, 1-5
Condition for Yahweh's help, 6-13
   First exhortation to fidelity, 6-8
   Motivation from grace: God-given success to date, 9-10
   Second exhortation to fidelity, 11
   Motivation from fear: God-inflicted disaster in the future, 12-13
Alternatives to Yahweh's help, 14-16
   (Yahweh is faithful in judgment as well as in grace)

This outline should make clear the drive of Joshua's address. It forms the background of our discussion, though I should like to survey the teaching under different headings. Let us now turn to the emphases Joshua has set before us.

The Peculiar Responsibility of Yahweh's Witnesses (23:1-3)
Observe, first of all, how Joshua stresses the peculiar responsibility of Yahweh's witnesses. Joshua sets himself in sharp contrast to Israel's leaders who remain: '*I* have become old, I have come into days [lit.], but *you* have seen all that Yahweh your God has done...' (vv. 2-3).[1] The burden of Joshua's exhortation to the leaders comes in verses 6-8: since they have actually seen Yahweh's work on behalf of Israel, they must be the spearheads of fidelity to him. It is a solemn time. Death is about to beckon Joshua; but he uses a last opportunity 'that he might leave the pure worship of God surviving him'.[2] These men who have both seen Yahweh's mighty work in the conquest and will outlive Joshua (24:31) bear a special responsibility to anchor Israel in spiritual faithfulness to the Lord and to spur Israel on to total occupation of the land;

---

[1] Note that the second half of the book opens with a notation about Joshua's age (13:1); here in 23:1-2 we have another near the close of the book.

[2] John Calvin, *Commentaries on the Book of Joshua*, trans. Henry Beveridge, in vol. 4 of *Calvin's Commentaries*, 22 vols. (reprint ed.; Grand Rapids: Baker 1981), 263. Calvin commends Joshua's practice as a model to fathers and rulers: 'The pious solicitude of Joshua is here also set forth, for the imitation of all who are in authority. For as the father of a family will not be considered sufficiently provident if he thinks of his children only till the end of his own life, and does not extend his care farther, studying as much as in him lies to do them good even when he is dead; so good magistrates and rulers ought carefully to provide that the well arranged condition of affairs as they leave them, be confirmed and prolonged to a distant period' (Ibid).

they must not allow any ecumenical movement to dilute and destroy Israel's distinctive faith and life (v. 7).

These leaders had seen all that Yahweh had done to 'all these nations' (v. 3) and 'had seen all Yahweh's great work which he had done for Israel' (Judg. 2:7); but the time will come when these witnesses will, like Joshua, leave the earthly struggle behind (Judg. 2:10a). It is at that point that we will hear of another generation 'who did not know Yahweh nor the work that he had done for Israel' (Judg. 2:10).[3] Does that mean Joshua's men had failed? Had they been lax in passing on the stories of Yahweh the warrior who conquered Canaan? We do not know, though Joshua 24:31 ('Now Israel served Yahweh all the days of Joshua and all the days of the elders who outlived Joshua') implies they were diligent rather than dilatory.

However, the fact that a faithless generation can arise out of the tracks of a faithful generation (see 23:8b on the latter) should impress us with how vital it is for one generation to, at least, pass on the amazing story of God's saving power and fearful judgment to the next, whether 'they hear or refuse to hear' (see Ezek. 2–3). While passing on the testimony of Yahweh's deeds cannot guarantee the fidelity of the next generation, the failure to pass it on will guarantee their unfaithfulness. Such is the burden of Psalm 78:

> I will utter dark sayings from of old,
> things that we have heard and known,
>   that our fathers have told us.
> We will not hide them from their children,
>   but tell to the coming generation
> the glorious deeds of the LORD, and his might,
>   and the wonders which he has wrought.
>
> He established a testimony in Jacob,
>   and appointed a law in Israel,
> which he commanded our fathers
>   to teach to their children;
> that the next generation might know them,

---

[3] I take 'did not know' (*lo' yad' u*) in Judges 2:10 to refer to a lack of confession rather than of cognition: not that they didn't know about Yahweh and his work, but that they refused to acknowledge such.

the children yet unborn,
and arise and tell them to their children,
    so that they should set their hope in God,
and not forget the works of God,
    but keep his commandments;
and that they should not be like their fathers,
    a stubborn and rebellious generation,
a generation whose heart was not steadfast,
    whose spirit was not faithful to God [Ps. 78:2b-8, RSV].[4]

There is a whole philosophy of covenant education. And it's not particularly the job of the church, but – if we heed the Book of Proverbs – of believing parents. We are to be witnesses in our own homes; doing or not doing this may determine whether our children or grandchildren 'set their hope in God' (Ps. 78:7).

We, too, as witnesses to God's grace, have a peculiar responsibility. Unlike Israel's leaders, we did not see what happened the moment the priests' feet touched the Jordan; we did not hear the roar of Jericho's crumbling walls; we did not hide in the ambush at Ai; we did not yell when the Beth-Horon bombs (Josh. 10:11) fell. But we have the record of it – even more than Israel's leaders had. None of it is boring or tedious or dull, as though the next generation would only yawn. What is dull about a God who became flesh? Who did what no one had ever done – perfectly kept God's law? Who became the God-forsaken One in my place? Who trampled all over death? Who reigns now over the universe? This faith we must teach to our children, for Canaan has all sorts of evangelists calling for decisions to fertility worship and sexual freedom.

The Confident Assurance of Yahweh's Help (23:3-5)
Secondly, Joshua underscores the confident assurance of Yahweh's help that Israel should have. He first refers to the relatively recent past: 'You have seen all that Yahweh your God has done to all these nations on account of you, for Yahweh your God – he is the one who has been fighting for you' (v. 3).[5]

---

[4] See also Psalm 44:1-3.
[5] The last verb, to fight, is in participial form, indicating continuing action. Among English versions only NASB and TEV bring this out. See Marten H. Woudstra, *The Book of Joshua*, The New International Commentary on the Old Testament (Grand Rapids: Eerdmans, 1981), 334.

Then he anticipates the immediate future: 'See! I have allotted to you all these remaining nations as an inheritance to your tribes.... Now Yahweh your God – he is the one who will thrust them out from before you, and he shall dispossess them from before you, and you shall possess their land, as Yahweh your God has promised you' (vv. 4-5).

Incidentally, we meet here the same consistent picture of the conquest that we find in all the extant biblical documents.[6] A decisive conquest (v. 3) and a continuing occupation (vv. 4-5); Yahweh has given rest (v. 1), yet there is still work (vv. 4-5). These two emphases are not contradictory but complementary. Indeed, God had disclosed from the first that there would be, of necessity, a gradual aspect in the conquest: 'I will not drive them out before you in one year; otherwise, the land would become desolate and the wild beasts multiply against you; little by little I will drive them out before you until you become fruitful and inherit the land' (Exod. 23:29-30).[7]

Joshua's object is not to explain the manner of the conquest but to furnish the basis for confidence. He wants those who remain to be sure of Yahweh's help. He grounds them in this assurance by appealing to Yahweh's recent activity (v. 3) and to his previous promise (v. 5; note: 'as Yahweh your God has promised you' refers to just such texts as Exod. 23:29-30). Both God's action and his word should support them. Anyone who had seen Yahweh in combat at Jericho, Ai, Beth-Horon, Merom, and Hazor should be able to trust him for the task that remains. And if God's promise had proven true to date, surely it was adequate for what lay ahead. Indeed Joshua does not stress Israel's bravado but exalts Yahweh's power: 'Yahweh your God – he is the one who has been fighting for you' (v. 3); 'Yahweh your God – he is the one who will thrust them out' (v. 5).

---

[6] By extant I mean the biblical documents as we have them, before someone carves them up into various 'sources' or 'traditions'.

[7] See similarly Deuteronomy 7:22, on which P. C. Craigie writes: 'The initial conquest would be sudden, but the process of settlement and complete conquest would be more gradual, while the Israelites grew sufficiently in number ... to enable them to populate the land.' To this he footnotes: 'Thus the verse anticipates the contrast between the book of Joshua and the statements at the beginning of Judges' (*The Book of Deuteronomy*, The New International Commentary on the Old Testament [Grand Rapids: Eerdmans, 1976], 182).

Such is, of course, the plain logic of faith. Here is the consistent biblical pattern. Israel's confidence and assurance spring from remembering Yahweh's faithful words and deeds in the past (see Pss. 105, 114, 135, 136) – the God who so acted them is surely adequate for what comes next. And such 'faithfull' reasoning seems to be what Jesus expects of his disciples as well – that if Christ feeds 5,000 men he can surely handle storms on the sea (see Mark 6:51b-52).

The Careful Obedience of Yahweh's People (23:6-13)

The bulk of chapter 23, however, concerns the careful obedience of Yahweh's people. Though Joshua may be addressing primarily the leaders (v. 2), he nevertheless addresses them as representatives of the people; thus what he demands of them he demands of every Israelite.

The Standard of Obedience

The standard of obedience is the Word of God.[8] 'Therefore stand firm to keep and fulfill all that is written in the Book of the Law of Moses, never turning aside from it to right or left' (v. 6, JB). In 1:7-8 this demand was laid upon Joshua; here he places all Israel under it. There is not some higher obedience required of God's 'full-time' (horrid phrase!) servants while the rest muddle along on a lower plane. All the Lord's people owe compliance to all the Lord's law.

The Form of Obedience

In verses 7-8 Joshua specifies the supreme obedience that the law of Moses requires. Israel is to live in accord with all that

---

[8] The Westminster Confession of Faith, chapter 16, stresses this point: 'Good works are only such as God hath commanded in his holy word, and no such as, without the warrant thereof, are devised by men out of blind zeal, or upon any pretense of good intention.' Scriptural obedience is demanding, but also liberating. Zealous Christian friends may tell you that you must spend time reading the Scriptures early in the morning. The Bible urges attention to God's word (e.g. Ps. 119), but it does not legislate that this must be early in the morning, perhaps against the metabolism of some, the wet diapers and breakfast preparations of others. Your eager Christian circle may push you to be faithful in spending thirty minutes at one time in prayer. Now the Bible commands Christ's disciples to pray (Matt. 6:5-8; Phil. 4:6-7), but it nowhere holds the stopwatch on us. Many Christians should think twice before they debunk the scribes and the Pharisees for *their* traditions.

the law of Moses demands (so says v. 6), and here is the most vital demand that the law requires (vv. 7-8):

> that you not have dealings with these nations that remain with you; and you must not call upon the name of their gods or swear by them; and you must not serve them or bow down to them; rather to Yahweh your God you are to cling.

Here then is the particular form of obedience; this obedience must take the form of separation. Having social mixers with the Canaanites will only make fertility theology more available to Israel and accommodation to the local beliefs seem more natural.

Separation remains the form of obedience for God's new covenant people. This may begin with the general demand to develop a Christian mind (e.g. 'Don't let the world around you squeeze you into its own mould, but let God re-mould your minds from within' [Rom. 12:2, *Phillips*]), but also embraces specific acts and decisions, such as seeking only a Christian companion in marriage (1 Cor. 7:39). How many have pierced themselves through with needless sorrows by trampling on this latter command! The application of obedient separation in Christian experience is frequently difficult and sometimes agonising (since many of us already have a passion for either laxity or legalism). But the difficulties or tensions do not negate the demand. We cannot be taken out of the world, but we must be kept from the evil one (cf. John 17:15).

Motives for Obedience

Frequently the Scriptures seek to move us to obedience by setting forth certain considerations, certain arguments, to bolster our will to obey. Jesus did this. No sooner had he said, 'If anyone would come after me, he must deny himself and take up his cross and follow me' (Mark 8:34, NIV) than he appends four arguments for meeting his demand (Mark 8:35-38). That is the pattern Joshua follows here: he asserts not only the standard and the form of obedience but the motives for obedience as well. In verses 9-10 he seeks to move Israel by the grace of God, while in verses 11-13 he appeals to the fear of God.

Verses 9-10 are reflective, summarising what Yahweh has done for Israel in the recent past: 'Yahweh has driven out from before you great and strong nations, and not a man has been able to stand against you to this day; one of your men chases a thousand, for Yahweh your God – he is the one fighting for you....' Hence, Israel's answer should be faithful obedience out of gratitude for Yahweh's recent goodness.

However, verses 11-13 are prospective – and threatening. If Israel turns away and clings not to Yahweh but to these remaining nations and intermarries with them, then Yahweh will no longer enable Israel to complete the conquest. Rather, these nations will prove to be 'as dangerous for you as a trap or a pit and as painful as a whip on your back or thorns in your eyes' (v. 13, TEV; see Num. 33:55).[9] And, at the last, Israel would perish from their good land.

Just as Joshua argues from the memory of Yahweh's goodness, so he appeals to the threat of Yahweh's judgment. Both the grace of God and the fear of God should move the people of God. There are those who would tell us that New Testament Christians (whatever they are) are no longer subject to the fear of God. But an afternoon with the Epistle to the Hebrews should effect a permanent cure.

The Utter Certainty of Yahweh's Judgment (23:14-16)

We continue with the element of threat and fear because Joshua does. He closes off his address, whether to our tastes or not, by emphasising the utter certainty of Yahweh's judgment.

At verse 14 Joshua hits the climax of his exhortation. He reminds those surviving him of what they knew so well – the thorough faithfulness of Yahweh: 'Not a single word has fallen of all the good words that Yahweh your God spoke about you; the whole has come about for you; not a single word of it has fallen' (see exposition of 21:43-45). What Yahweh has said he has fulfilled in detail. Excellent! Now it is time for the benediction. But Joshua has not yet made his point. 'And it shall be,' he continues, 'that just as all the benefits that Yahweh your God has promised to you have come upon you,

---

[9] The imagery of the trap and pit suggests that Israel will not be aware of how deadly pagan fellowship is until too late. Such is the 'deceitfulness of sin' (Heb. 3:13).

so too Yahweh will bring upon you all the disasters until he exterminates you from upon this good land that Yahweh your God has given you' (v. 15).[10] Such divine disaster would come should Israel break the covenant by serving and worshipping other gods, as verse 16 explains.

What an impact! After verse 14 we are ready to stand and sing, in our finest devotional mood, 'Great Is Thy Faithfulness'. But before we can strike the chord, Joshua preaches to us that Yahweh's faithfulness is a two-edged sword (v. 15), that he is faithful both in grace and in judgment. Yahweh's fidelity is not displayed just in covenant blessing but in covenant judgment as well, by which he testifies that he has not let go of his people but pursues them even in their sins. We do not have a tame, safe God, but one who is faithful to heal and destroy. Unlike Santa Claus, Yahweh is holy and his threats are not empty gobbledygook.

One can tell Joshua had had little exposure to homiletics (Moses' discipling was perhaps deficient on that score), or he wouldn't have concluded his remarks on such a negative, jarring note. Psychologically, it would have been better had he somehow concluded with verse 14 on a positive note. As it is, the chapter begins with Yahweh's rest (v. 1) and closes, thanks to Joshua, with Yahweh's anger (v. 16).

We see this pattern elsewhere in Scripture. We become excited listening to the psalmist depict the greatness of God in Psalm 95:1-5; we are warmed as we hear him speak of the nearness of this great God in verses 6-7c; then we are shocked as God himself interrupts with an alarm about our hardness of heart (Ps. 95:7d-11). All of which suggests that God will even ruin a psalm if it will wake us up to our unbelief and hardness of heart. So this is not just Joshua's negativism.

---

[10] It seems to be a scholarly assumption that any allusions to Israel's being driven or destroyed from the land must presuppose the (Babylonian) exile. Thus Soggin holds that Joshua 23:13-16 is a *vaticnium ex eventu*; that is, the verses were written after the Babylonian exile had occurred and were put into Joshua's mouth as though they were a prediction of a future event (J. Alberto Soggin, *Joshau: A Commentary*, Old Testament Library [Philadelphia: Westminster, 1972], 218-19). The assumption is that one could hardly mention the threat of exile unless he had actually experienced it; which makes as much sense as saying that someone from south Florida could not mention snow because he had never seen it. For a succinct critique of this error, see Kenneth A. Kitchen, 'Ancient Orient, "Deuteronism," and the Old Testament', in *New Perspectives on the Old Testament*, ed. J. Baron Payne (Waco: Word, 1970), 5-7.

When I was in fifth and sixth grades, our school system switched to the vogue of dispensing with A-B-C grades and went to a system of S and U (satisfactory and unsatisfactory), with plus and minus thrown in. This somewhat irked my father and so when on one occasion he signed my report card, he registered his disgust with the new scheme and wrote in the comment section, 'Why is giving an exact grade sinful?'

Now that is the point here. Why is a negative ending sinful? Because it will make Israel feel badly about themselves? What difference does that make? We may not prefer unhappy endings, but there is nothing wrong with an unhappy ending if it leads us to faithfulness. Always the Scriptures hold before us both 'the kindness and the severity of God' (Rom. 11:22); we forget either one to our peril.

At this point we probably sit back, reflecting, with just a bit of a smile playing at our gentile faces, and begin to say to our souls, 'Well, yes, that was Israel for you, seldom faithful, always needing judgment; but I'm a Christian and....' Wait! Don't cross over the line from biblical faith to gentile conceit. Remember where you are – hanging as a graft on God's Jewish olive tree (see Rom. 11). Some of the natural Jewish branches were broken off because of unbelief, 'but you stand fast only by faith' (Rom. 11:20). So, no smirks; sackcloth, ashes, and awe are due, for 'if God did not spare the natural branches, neither will he spare you' (Rom. 11:21). Beware of thinking that Joshua 23 carries only Israel's address.

Study Questions:

1. How important is it that we pass on to the next generation the 'praise worthy deeds of our God?'

2. Why are believers so prone to forget in the present what Yahweh has done in the past?

3. Why does scripture remind believers so often to 'remember?'

4. Does the fear of God move you to obedience or does it cause you to be afraid to do anything?

5. Is it wrong to be scared to obedience? Why does God give such warnings in the middle of praise?

21

Covenant Renewal
at Abraham's Place
(Joshua 24:1-28)

Here we are in Shechem, rubbing shoulders with various elders, judges, leaders of Israel, participating in the third assembly of God's people at the close of the Book of Joshua (see on ch. 22), and feeling solemn, for it's a solemn occasion: we are standing 'before God' (v. 1) and we are about to hear Yahweh's word (v. 2a).[1] It's a historic, sacred moment. One feels both cold and warm at once. Who can describe how

---

[1] Much ink has been justly spilled on Joshua 24 as a covenant renewal ceremony and on whether and to what degree the chapter fits into the literary pattern of various ancient Near Eastern treaties that have come to light. A normal outline for a second millennium BC Hittiite treaty would be: (1) preamble, identifying the king ordaining the covenant; (2) historical prologue, reviewing the king's past benefits to the subject party; (3) stipulations, that is, the demands (basic and/or detailed) that the king places upon his vassal(s); (4) provisions relating to the document of the treaty, where it is to be placed and when read; (5) witnesses, frequently consisting of pagan gods; and (6) curses and blessings, for faithlessness or fidelity to the treaty. Since Joshua 24 is not the precise text of the covenant/treaty but a report of the covenant renewal, one need not expect to find the exact treaty pattern. But there are recognisable elements of it: (1) preamble (v. 2, 'Thus says Yahweh, the God of Israel'); (2) historical prologue, verses 2b-13; (3) stipulation – basic, verses 14-15; (4) document provision, verse 26; (5) witnesses, verses 22, 26b-27; and (6) curses, cf. verses 19-20. The first three elements follow the usual order. For a succinct review of the treaty form and its importance, see Kenneth A. Kitchen, *The Bible in Its World: The Bible and Archaeology Today* (Downers Grove: Inter-Varsity, 1977), 79-85; see also his *Ancient Orient and Old Testament* (Chicago: Inter-Varsity, 1966), 90-102.

one of the seed of Abraham must feel standing in Abraham's Place? The reader may try his or her own comparisons. For me, I should think the effect would be like visiting Scotland and frequenting the haunts of my historical heroes, Andrew and Horatius Bonar, Rabbi Duncan, and Robert Murray McCheyne.

In seeking to hear the theological witness of the text, I would like to divide the text structurally into its three broad sections (vv. 2-13, 14-24, 25-28) and develop each of these divisions – particularly the first – in some detail.

The Review of Covenant History (24:2-13)

In verses 2-13 we hear Joshua proclaim the review of covenant history. His survey centres upon crisis points in Israel's history, on threats to Israel's welfare, each of which is met by Yahweh's intervention. We easily miss the fact that this is a history that should never have happened. Only the grace and power of Yahweh explain why there was now an Israel to stand at Shechem and listen to a Joshua.[2] So Joshua rehearses the story of the King's grace, which corresponds to the historical prologue of the ancient treaties. And what a prologue Yahweh has created!

The Surprising Grace of God

Covenant history begins with the surprising grace of God: 'A long time ago your fathers lived beyond the river, Terah, the father of Abraham and Nahor, and they served other gods; then I took your father Abraham...' (vv. 2b-3a). We should not run around the plain implication of the text – that Abraham was plunged into pagan worship just as the rest: 'They served other gods.' 'But if we attend to the words of the inspired writer, we shall see that he [Abraham] is no more exempted from the guilt of the popular idolatry than Terah and Nachor.'[3]

Yet there is a persistent tendency in the popular Christian mind to look upon folks like Abraham as if they had always

---

[2] Cf. Karl Gutbrod's comments on Israel as 'the miracle of history'; *Das Buch vom Lande gottes*, Die Botschaft des Alten Testaments, 3d. ed. (Stuttgart: Calwer, 1965), 158.

[3] John Calvin, *Commentaries on the Book of Joshua*, trans. Henry Beveridge, in vol. 4 of *Calvin's Commentaries*, 22 vols. (reprint ed.; Grand Rapids: Baker, 1981), 272.

been a Mr. Goodwrench – good, solid, helpful folks to whom no God who had an ounce of wisdom could avoid taking a shine. Nor could some Jewish minds quite stand it. The pseudepigraphal book of Jubilees pictures Abram at fourteen understanding the error of pagan worship and separating 'from his father so that he might not worship the idols with him' (Jub. 11:16). Indeed he exhorts his father to dump idols and worship the God of heaven (Jub. 12:1-8). However, when he is sixty, Abram really gets drastic and burns the house of idols (Jub. 12:12-14).

All of which goes to show that John Newton was right: grace really is amazing. So amazing that we can't believe it. So we go on concocting our graven images of biblical all-stars, like Abraham, picturing them as worthy fellows already disposed toward God, already on the way to truth, needing only a little help from God to finish a conversion so nobly begun.

But it is all rubbish. 'They served other gods.' That is the situation of Abraham. 'Then I took your father Abraham.' That is the grace of Yahweh. It all started there – in unexpected, unimaginable, unexplainable grace. Abraham rose out of the desolate pit and miry bog of paganism only because Yahweh touched him. 'Abraham did not emerge from profound ignorance and the abyss of error by his own virtue, but was drawn out by the hand of God.'[4] That there is a people of God at all hangs on the single thread of the mere good pleasure of God, who, for no apparent reason, took hold of our father Abraham, the sinner.

The Gradual Pace of God

We don't live long in covenant history until we experience the gradual pace of God. Still speaking of Abraham, Joshua continues Yahweh's word: 'and I multiplied his seed and I gave him Isaac' (v. 3b). Those two statements look ludicrous together. God multiplies Abraham's seed – he gives him Isaac. One times one is one. And, according to the mathematics of Genesis, it took twenty-five years just to get Isaac (Gen. 12:4; 16:3, 16; 17:1, 17; 21:5).

---

[4] Ibid., 273.

But perhaps we should have allowed Joshua to go on: 'I multiplied his seed, and I gave him Isaac, and I gave Isaac Jacob and Esau' (vv. 3b-4a). That's not much better. Yahweh multiplies Abraham's seed by giving him two grandsons! And, according to the scriptural math, that was after twenty years of childlessness for Isaac and Rebekah (Gen. 25:19-26).

God does not appear to be in a hurry; he is not driven by the calendar or intimidated by the clock. Yahweh did multiply Abraham's seed but he did it slowly. He does what he promises but sometimes so gradually that we don't see his faithfulness. This is frequently God's way – to be 'faithful in little' and even little by little. It might help our faith if we would fasten our eyes more on the fact than the degree of God's faithfulness, or its speed. We easily lose sight of what Yahweh has done by demanding too much too soon.

Every time I enter the print shop in town, I see a poster the proprietors have prominently displayed behind the counter. There are three cartoonlike characters on it, in various positions, laughing wildly and holding their sides. The caption reads: 'You want it when?!' It's a subtle message to impatient customers who think their order should have been ready the day before they brought it in. Perhaps it's more of a parable than a poster for those of us who chafe at the pace of God's faithfulness.

The Mystifying Ways of God

One twister leads to another: in covenant history sooner or later we encounter the mystifying ways of God. 'I gave Esau Mt. Seir to possess, but Jacob and his sons went down to Egypt' (v. 4b).[5]

Now why is that? Why do Esau and his family, the non-covenant line, get their inheritance, while the covenant family (Jacob and Co.) do not receive theirs – indeed, they go to Egypt where, eventually, they will be enslaved (Gen. 15:13-16)? Why do the covenant people experience hardship and slavery

---

[5] Mount Seir traditionally refers to the territory of Edom (Esau's descendants) south/southeast of the Dead Sea, east of the Arabah. But the term may include territory to the west of the Arabah as well. For an introduction to the question, the reader may check John D. W. Watts, 'Seir', *Wycliffe Bible Encyclopedia*, 2 vols. (Chicago: Moody, 1975), 2:1545; and Andrew Bowling, 'Seir', *ZPEB*, 5:329-30.

while others have their reward? Why do God's chosen ones experience the affliction while others enjoy their good things? See how Scripture recognises this mystery, that God's people so often have to wait in great distress for God's promised blessing?[6]

This total candor of Scripture about the life of faith is so refreshing. Hebrews 11:32-38 illustrates this perfectly. That writer makes no bones about the astounding benefits God gives to faith: his people conquered kingdoms, shut lions' mouths, escaped the sword, routed alien armies, observed resurrections (Heb. 11:32-35a). Now that is the victorious Christian life! That's what God does for his people who believe! Yet the writer continues with nary a semicolon: 'Others were tortured ... some faced jeers and flogging ... they were stoned; they were sawed in two ... put to death by the sword ... went about in sheepskins and goatskins, destitute, persecuted and mistreated ... they wandered in deserts and mountains, and in caves and holes in the ground' (Heb. 11:35b-38, NIV). That's what God does for his people who believe. Thus the writer makes no bones about the strange hardships God allows to faith. Is that the 'victorious Christian life'? Who knows? But it's as much the Christian life as conquering kingdoms and muzzling lions.

My point is that neither Scripture nor God speaking in Scripture glosses over this mystery. Back to Joshua 24:4. Even in this overall survey of Yahweh's goodness to Israel we find this mystery. Esau received his possession; Jacob and his family went down to Egypt. The mystery must be seen both in and in light of the whole story. Weeping *may* endure for the night (cf. Ps. 30:4-5).

There is no use kicking at this mystery, but the mystery itself should lead us to adore our God. Why? Because when he rehearses the story of his grace he doesn't hide the (to us) rough spots; he doesn't gloss over the perplexities; he doesn't

---

[6] Marten H. Woudstra (*The Book of Joshua*, The New International Commentary on the Old Testament [Grand Rapids: Eerdmans, 1981], 346) comments on verse 4: 'Thus, while election was stressed at the beginning of the verse, the course of history, which often seems to conflict with God's design, also is given ample recognition. In Egypt Jacob and his descendants would appear for centuries to be anything but the elect people of God, suffering cruelly as they did at the hands of Egypt's kings.'

omit the difficulties. He never erases the mysteries or dark times from the record. My point is, you can trust a God like that. Here is a straightforward, honest God.

One reason why I believe the New Testament record of the resurrection of Jesus is because Matthew's Gospel contains three words in relating the disciples' meeting with the risen Lord in Galilee: 'But some doubted' (Matt. 28:17). Someone might ask, 'How can hearing of their doubt support your faith?' Simply because it tells me that the writer has nothing to hide. If Matthew was trying to feed me theological baloney he would have suppressed mention of anyone – especially among Jesus' followers – doubting Jesus and his resurrection. The fact that he so candidly and openly notes it tells me that Matthew (or, if you prefer, the writer of the first Gospel) has nothing to hide, no secrets to keep; I can trust a man like that to tell me the truth.

And such is our God. He is kind enough to show us plainly that within the story of his grace we may meet with darkness. Not that we will relish the darkness. But a God that truthful can be trusted to hold us in the darkness.

The Manifest Power of God
As expected, a substantial section of this historical prologue recounts the manifest power of God. Joshua outlines three major moments of that power:

Deliverance from Egypt, 5-7
    Sending of human instruments, 5a
    Infliction of the plagues, 5b
    Rescue at the sea, 6-7
Conquest east of the Jordan, 8
(see Num. 21:21-35)
Conquest west of the Jordan, 11-12
    Victory at Jericho, 11
    Victory over 'two kings of the Amorites', 12[7]

---

[7] I take the two kings of the Amorites in verse 12 to refer to the ringleaders of the southern and northern coalitions, namely, Adonizedek and Jabin resepctively (see 10:3, 5; 11:1-3) and not as a misplaced reference to Sihon and Og (v. 8; Num. 21). Cf. Alan R. Millard, 'Amorites', *IBD*, 1:43-44. No one knows for certain what the hornet (v. 12) refers to (see also Exod. 23:27-28; Deut. 7:20), whether to literal hornets, or to

The major impression Israel is to receive from this section is that the power is solely Yahweh's. Joshua makes the point deftly at the end of verse 12, summing up the conquest west of the Jordan: 'it was not by your sword or by your bow' (see Ps. 44:3, 5-7).[8] Don't begin to imagine that your own efforts achieved this. The praise belongs to Yahweh and his strong arm.

The 'rescue at the sea' section (vv. 6-7) preaches the same point.

> I brought your fathers out of Egypt and you came to the sea; and the Egyptians pursued your father with chariots and horsemen to the Red Sea; then they began to cry out to Yahweh and he placed darkness between you and the Egyptians; then he brought the sea over them – it covered them and your eyes saw what I did against the Egyptians.[9]

That is Exodus 14 in concentrate. And Exodus 14 stresses the utter helplessness of Israel at the sea. In fact, it says that Yahweh himself placed them in that position of helplessness. Even though there is no certainty about precisely where Pi-ha-hiroth, Migdol, and Baal-Zephon (Exod. 14:2) were located, the general description in Exodus 14:1-4 allows us to see the picture. Israel was going out the exit and Yahweh ordered them to 'turn back' and camp 'between Migdol and the sea'

---

dread and panic, or to Egyptian campaigns in Canaan (cf. Woudstra, *Joshua*, 349). Calvin (*Joshua*, 274), however, has seized the main concern: 'But when the thing is effected by hornets, the divine agency is inudubitably asserted. Accordingly, the conclusion is, that the people did not acquire the land by their own sword or bow....'

[8] George Bush (*Notes, Critical and Practical, on the Book of Joshua* [Chicago: Henry A. Sumner, 1881], 212) clarifies: 'Not that these implements were not made use of in their wars, but that they would have used them in vain unless God, by his secret or open judgments, had previously smitten and paralysed the power of the enemy.'

[9] Note the constant shifting between 'your fathers' and 'you' in these verses. Yahweh brought 'your fathers' out of Egypt, but 'you came to the sea'. The fathers cried out, but God placed darkness 'between you and the Egyptians'; 'your eyes saw' what God did to the Egyptians. In one sense 'you came to the sea' was strictly accurate, for many of those who had experienced the exodus and were under twenty years of age at the time of the rebellion in the wilderness (see Num. 14:28-31) would have been standing before Joshua at Shechem. However, Joshua's 'you' may also reflect the contemporising of Yahweh's covenant dealings; that is, what Yahweh has done for our fathers we (a later generation) are to regard as having been done for us. See, for example, Deuteronomy 5:2-3. God's grace is both historical and contemporary, both age-old and ever-fresh.

(14:2). Pharaoh would then think that Israel was 'wandering around the land in confusion, hemmed in by the desert' (14:3, NIV). It appears that Yahweh deliberately placed Israel as sitting ducks by the sea for Pharaoh; they were hemmed in and totally helpless as Egypt's military machines rolled in behind them.

Why does God operate that way? To show, in a word, that salvation is of the Lord (Jonah 2:9); 'to make it clear that such an overwhelming power comes from God and not from us' (2 Cor. 4:7, JB); to insist that 'there is no place for human pride in the presence of God' (1 Cor. 1:29, NEB). Don't misunderstand; God's purpose is not to deform us into blobs of limp jello who only let go and let God, but to transform us into humble worshippers who gladly confess our 'help comes from Yahweh, maker of heaven and earth' (Ps. 121:2). God will sometimes box us up in our own helplessness in order to show us we are not delivered by our own cleverness, insight, manipulation, or anxiety, but by Yahweh 'who makes a way in the sea, a path in the mighty waters' (Isa. 43:16, RSV).

The Faithful Protection of God

In verses 9-10 Joshua alludes to the Balaam episode, reminding Israel of the faithful protection of God. You may refer to Numbers 22–24 (plus Num. 25 and 31:8, 14-16) to review the whole story, though Joshua gives the essence of it.

Israel had arrived at the plains of Moab, ready to enter Canaan. Balak, king of Moab, hired Balaam, a most successful diviner, to come curse Israel. Balaam was to put the hokey-pokey, lickety-split on Israel, so that Balak could defeat them in battle. Balaam was a prophet for profit and, though God at last permitted him to go to Balak, he made it clear that Balaam could do only what God directed or allowed (Num. 22:20), which might make it difficult for Balaam to be successful in collecting his check.

So that Balaam would realise just how much he was under Yahweh's control, God gave him extra tutoring on his journey to Moab. Three times the angel of Yahweh stands in the road ready to plunge his sword through Balaam. And on each occasion Balaam's ass is his saviour – and gets punished for it.

The ass went off into a field, smashed Balaam's foot against a vineyard wall (better one foot crushed than a sword through your middle), and finally lay down on the job (Num. 22:22-27). While Balaam was beating the daylights out of her, his ass asked what she had done to deserve such abuse. The Israelites knew that asses don't talk and that's why Numbers 22:28 states that 'Yahweh opened the mouth of the ass.' It was an act of God. If God must make an ass talk to get Balaam's attention, he must have been pretty dense.

Then, as Yahweh had opened the ass's mouth, he opened Balaam's eyes (Num. 22:31), and Balaam saw he was within an inch of death. Here is real irony. Balaam is the diviner, the seer, the one who perceives. Yet it was the ass who saw the angel of Yahweh while Balaam did not. The dumb ass was sharper than Balaam. Though some may take offence, we can truthfully say that the point of the narrative is that Balaam is the real ass.

The scrape with death evidently sobered Balaam and he got Yahweh's point: 'Go with the men; but only the word which I bid you, that shall you speak' (Num. 22:35, RSV). Balaam's lucrative heart longed to curse Israel, but he was held in God's vise grips. It is an awesome, helpless feeling – to be held in the crunch of Shaddai's hand. He could speak only Yahweh's will. And Yahweh's will was blessing for Israel.

The rest is history (see Num. 23–24). Balak had amassed all the brass, pomp, and regalia (and maybe several high-school bands) to hear Balaam's magic curse. But every attempt brought only Balaamic blessing. Just as Yahweh says in Joshua's summary (back to Josh. 24): 'But I did not want to listen to Balaam, so he kept on blessing you, and I delivered you from his hand' (v. 10).[10] (The whole episode in Numbers 22–24 must be viewed in light of Genesis 12:3a, 'I will bless those who bless you, and the one who curses you I will curse.' This is the protection clause of Yahweh's promise to Abraham, and it should control our reading of Numbers 22–24. Yahweh's will

---

[10] The Hebrew construction with an infinitive absolute following its cognate verb indicates continued action; hence *wayebarek barok* is translated 'he kept on blessing you'. See J. Wash Watts, *A Survey of Syntax in the Hebrew Old Testament* (Grand Rapids: Eerdmans, 1964), 92-93.

for Abraham and seed is blessing and, Balaam or no Balaam, he will bless them.)

So Joshua preaches to Israel, 'Remember the faithful protection of God; remember how he shielded you from Balaam's passion and Balak's purpose.' The same appeal applies to God's people in every age. The Balaams and Balaks assume different guises but the protection of God remains unchanging. Jesus says as much of his church: 'I will build my church, and the powers of death shall not prevail against it' (Matt. 16:18, rsv). The same holds for God's people individually, though many of us have sometimes wondered where God's shielding hand was in our tragedy and losses. But my knowledge and yours is too fragmentary. If you knew what God has kept you from and what he has kept from you, you would have no trouble confessing how faithful his protection has been.

The Continuous Provision of God

The story of amazing grace includes the continuous provision of God. We have a hint of this in verse 7: 'and you lived in the wilderness a long time' (rsv). What a load is packed into that clause! Half of Exodus and all of Numbers are compacted into those words. Their mere survival from Egypt to Canaan was nothing less than one long miracle.

However, Israel was now enjoying Yahweh's abundant provision in the land of promise: 'And I gave you a land you did not toil for and cities you did not build – and you began to live in them; you are now eating from vineyards and olive trees you did not plant' (v. 13). Here is abundant provision and it too flows from grace ('I gave'); there is nothing automatic about it.

Combine the testimony of verses 7 and 13. Here is provision in necessity (v. 7) and in abundance (v. 13). But each is God's provision and all is God's sustenance. And please note how very earthy Yahweh's provision is: whether manna in the wilderness or vineyards in Canaan, it is food for covenant stomachs; it is land on which to settle and towns in which to have homes. Towns to live in and produce for food. How crass and unspiritual can we get? But God's people never get

beyond that: daily bread and corn flakes and casseroles are
the stuff for which Jesus teaches us to pray (Matt. 6:11).

Such is the review of covenant history, the story of the
King's grace. Do you begin to feel the gentle handcuffs of
God's goodness slipping around the wrists of your heart? He
says: 'Remember how I took you as my own; how I baffled
you, rescued you in your helplessness; how I shielded you
from dangers seen and unseen; how I have sustained you with
bread and meat until this very day.' 'Oh, to grace, how great
a debtor, daily I'm constrained to be!' Do you feel the claim of
this text, the pull it exerts upon your affections?

Of course, since our God is ever adding 'grace on top of
grace' (John 1:16), the historical prologue of his benefits gets
longer and more amazing. Above all, the story of the King's
grace now includes the act of the King's sacrifice. You can
no longer be your own, 'for you were bought with a price'
(1 Cor. 6:19-20). You now lead a life of innovative holiness
and trembling awe, 'knowing as you do that you were not
ransomed from your empty way of life ... with perishable
stuff – silver or gold, but with precious blood ... even Christ's'
(1 Peter 1:14-19). The logic of these New Testament texts
presses the claim of grace upon us. This claim and call and
argument of God's grace explains so much. It explains why
Galatians 2:20 is such a long verse. Paul tried to stop with the
words 'Son of God' but couldn't. He couldn't help himself;
he had to add 'who loved me and gave himself for me'. It
explains why the 'immortal, invisible' of 1 Timothy 1:17 is not
so much doxological filler; it is the response of one who is
utterly astounded at the overflowing grace of the Lord Jesus
toward a vicious blasphemer who remains the foremost of
sinners. God's goodness comes equipped with fetters and his
people are glad to be its captives.[11]

The Demand for Covenant Commitment (24:14-24)

In the second major section of the text Joshua presses the
demand for covenant commitment (vv. 14-24) upon Israel.

---

[11] Our discussion has centred upon the canonical acts of Yahweh's grace.
However, the individual believer will find it useful to compile the key moments of
God's grace in his or her own life and circumstances through the years.

These verses contain four statements by Joshua and four responses by Israel:

> Joshua – demand, 14-15
> > Israel – decision, 16-18
>
> Joshua – caution, 19-20
> > Israel – insistence, 21
>
> Joshua – query, 22a
> > Israel – acknowledgment, 22b
>
> Joshua – demand, 23
> > Israel – reaffirmation, 24

A Logical Commitment

What sort of commitment does the covenant call for? It demands a logical commitment: 'And now fear Yahweh and serve him in whole-heartedness and fidelity' (v. 14a). The 'and now' places the response demanded in light of the grace displayed (vv. 2-13). Fidelity to Yahweh is but the natural contemporary response to his abundant historical goodness. What else could one do toward a God who calls, delivers, protects, and supplies? There is a compulsion about it. It is the only reasonable response to overwhelming waves of Yahweh's mercies. Israel is held in the grip of grace; they are almost coerced to faithfulness by sheer logic. We have, quite expectedly, the same pattern in the New Testament. As stated before, it is in light of the lavish mercies of God depicted in Romans 1–11 that Romans 12:1-2 calls believers to their only rational response:

> So then, my brothers, in view of all these mercies that God has bestowed on you, I now make this plea. Present your bodies to God, present them as a sacrifice – a living one, not a lifeless one; a holy one (because it is offered to a holy God), and one in which He will take pleasure. For, when you consider your indebtedness to God, the consecration of your lives to His service is your logical act of worship.[12]

I was going to say that the Christian's response to God is bloodlessly rational. But it can never be bloodlessly rational,

---

[12] F. F. Bruce, *An Expanded Paraphrase of the Epistles of Paul* (Exeter: Paternoster, 1965), 223, 225.

can it? Not for a Christian. Rational, certainly, but bloodlessly
rational, never.

An Exclusive Commitment

Then Joshua also demands an exclusive commitment (vv. 14b-15;
see also v. 23):

> ... and put away the gods your fathers served beyond the river
> and in Egypt and serve Yahweh. And if you do not want to serve
> Yahweh, choose today whom you are going to serve – whether
> the gods your fathers served beyond the river or the gods of the
> Amorites in whose land you are living. But I and my house, we
> are going to serve Yahweh.

There is no doubt about what Joshua is after. That word *serve*
(Hebrew, *'abad*) appears seven times in these two verses (the
Hebrew root is like measles in ch. 24, occurring eighteen
times). Israel must decide whose slaves they will be (cf.
Rom. 6:17-18, 22).

Joshua appears to do a strange thing. Not every one
notices that his famous choose-you-this-day command calls
Israel to choose between two sets of pagan gods! Back up.
Joshua calls Israel to 'serve Yahweh' (v. 14). But if Israel will
not serve Yahweh, they must at least choose some god(s). He
presses Israel to the wall; they must come down somewhere.
If not Yahweh, the real historical God, then they must choose
either the ancestral Mesopotamian gods or the contemporary
Amorite ones. The conservatives who were fond of tradition,
of what had stood the test of time, who yearned for the 'faith
of our fathers', might vote for Mesopotamia. The liberals with
their yen for relevance, for being in step with the times, might
prefer to identify (as an act of goodwill) with the current
social milieu and enter into dialogue and worship with the
Amorites. But you must choose; if not Yahweh, then take your
pick from 'these dunghill deities' (Matthew Henry).

Some may be disturbed at the way evangelist Joshua calls
for decisions. Is he serious about which pagan gods they
should choose? How could that really be a choice? I think that
is precisely Joshua's point. He is using a reductio ad absurdum.
He says, 'Serve Yahweh; but if you won't, choose which non-

gods you will serve.' You will say, 'But that's stupid; choosing between pagan gods is really absurd.' Joshua retorts: 'That's precisely my point. If you reject Yahweh, you are stupid, and the only options left are so absurd that they make no sense at all.' This approach baffles our prosaic western minds. But Joshua is not driving Israel from Yahweh's service but seeking to shock them into being his slaves forever. And sometimes shock treatments work better than predictable preaching.

In any case, no matter what Israel does, Joshua has taken his stand: 'But I and my house, we are going to serve Yahweh' (v. 15b).[13] Popular opinion may differ; it makes no difference. Here is where I come down – no matter what.

Joshua pushes Israel in his own creative way to an either/ or commitment. If they are going to serve Yahweh, then they must 'put away the foreign gods among [them]' (v. 23). It is all or nothing. Israel must give themselves completely to Yahweh or not at all. It is the hog's dilemma in that hackneyed hog and hen story. Both hen and hog were walking past a church and noted the pastor's sermon title on the outside bulletin board. It read: 'What can we do to help the poor?' As hogs and hens are wont to do, they entered into earnest conversation over the question as they continued on their way. At last, the hen was smitten with a bright idea: 'I've got it,' she cackled, 'we can help the poor by giving them a ham and eggs breakfast!' 'Oh no you don't,' shot back the hog, 'for you, that only means a contribution, but for me, it means total commitment.' The old sow was right. That is Joshua's point – there can be no chicken's way out, but Israel must go whole hog (if one may so speak) for Yahweh. No compromise on this point. They must consider whose slaves they will be.

---

[13] Delbert R. Hillers (*Covenant: The History of a Biblical Idea* [Baltimore: Johns Hopkins, 1969], 63) holds that Joshua's decision reveals that 'entrance into this covenant with Yahweh was a matter for each individual family to decide.... God's covenant was, of course, not [here] with the head of the Israelite state, nor was it possible as far as we can tell for one tribal leader to commit a whole tribe. The sacred pact was concluded with individual families, and it remained the responsibility of each father to acquaint his children with its provisions.' Christian fathers should chew on this.

A Cautious Commitment

One could hardly have asked for a more gratifying and orthodox response than what Joshua received from Israel in verses 16-18:

> Far be it from us to forsake Yahweh to serve other gods! For Yahweh our God is the one who brought us and our fathers up from the land of Egypt, from the house of slaves, and who did these great signs before our eyes, who preserved us in all the way in which we have traveled and among all the people among whom we passed, and who drove out before us all the peoples, particularly the Amorites who live in the land. Yes, we too are going to serve Yahweh, for he is our God.

To Joshua's 'I and my house' (v. 15) they add their 'we too'. But then Joshua does something no decision-loving evangelist should ever do. To Israel's 'we too' he opposes his 'you cannot' (v. 19). If Israel gives herself to Yahweh it must be in a cautious commitment.

Joshua's is a shocking refusal. 'You cannot serve Yahweh, for he is a holy God; he is a jealous God; he will not go on forgiving your rebellion and your sins' (v. 19). If you desert him, he will consume you (v. 20). Don't lightly mouth your profession of faith, Joshua is saying. Don't you realise the sort of God you are dealing with? He is a holy, jealous God. You don't dare come to him thinking, 'though it makes him sad to see the way we live, he'll always say, "I forgive"'. Yahweh is not a soft, cuddly Santa in the sky who drools over easy decisions during invitation hymns. Joshua seeks to put down that blathering self-confidence that makes emotional commitments rather than shutting its mouth and counting the cost.

'You cannot serve Yahweh.' Neither Israel nor the church could hear a more beneficial word than that.

It was precisely when the Jesus bandwagon was going great guns (Luke 14:25) that Jesus emphasised who 'cannot be my disciple' (Luke 14:26, 27, 33). Rather, one must carefully 'count the cost' (Luke 14:28) before yielding allegiance to Jesus. The church should note this. Too frequently, the Jesus we present is some variety of prepackaged joy, peace, and provision that works twice as fast as aspirin. He is our cellophane Christ. We should not sell Christ like that but warn people about him! Our task is not to bait people into saying, 'I will lay down my life for you' (John 13:37), but to get them (and ourselves) to squirm under his searching, 'Do you love me?' (John 21:15-19). Too many of us perjure ourselves before a holy Judge as we sing, 'I surrender all', or 'My Jesus, I love thee'. There are stanzas in some hymns that I dare not sing.

One of the healthiest things a Christian can do is to doubt and question his easy expressions of commitment. One of the ordination vows my denomination asks of me is:

> Do you engage to be faithful and diligent in the exercise of all your duties as a Christian and a minister of the Gospel, whether personal or relational, private or public; and to endeavor by the grace of God to adorn the profession of the Gospel in your manner of life, and to walk with exemplary piety before the flock of which God shall make you overseer?

I would not touch that with the proverbial ten-foot pole. It asks too much of a proud, angry, lustful, covetous man. I affirm it only because there is that clause, 'by the grace of God', in it. Otherwise, I would have to turn away, for it would be too much to promise. Baptismal, membership, and marriage vows should receive the same scrutiny.

We must retain Joshua's paradox, must constantly stand between his 'serve Yahweh' (v. 14) and his 'you cannot serve Yahweh' (v. 19). His purpose is not to drive us from Yahweh but to him.[14] Only we must not make our commitment easily, lightly, flippantly, casually, but cautiously and fearfully (vv. 21, 24).

---

[14] Calvin (*Joshua*, 276) nicely catches the thrust of verse 19: 'What follows is still more absurd, when he tells them that they cannot serve the Lord, as if he were actually desirous of set purpose to impel them to shake off the yoke. But there is no doubt that his tongue was guided by the inspiration of the Spirit, in stirring up and disclosing their feelings. For when the Lord brings men under his authority, they are usually willing enough to profess zeal for piety, though they instantly fall away from it. Thus they build without a foundation. This happens because they neither distrust their own weakness so much as they ought, nor consider how difficult it is to bind

The Wonder of Covenant Religion (24:25-28)

In the third section of the text we can observe the wonder of covenant religion. Now in one sense there is no wonder here at all. These verses contain certain predictable elements of covenant and treaty ratification. There was, evidently, the customary sacrifice, for that seems implied in the language of verse 25a, 'So Joshua cut a covenant with/for the people on that day.'[15] There was the written document, for 'Joshua wrote down these words in the book of the torah of God' (v. 26a).[16] And then there stands a silent witness – a huge stone (vv. 26b-27)! It may seem spooky to read of a stone that has heard all the words that Yahweh spoke that day.[17] (Do rocks have ears?) But in pagan treaties the various gods are summoned as witnesses. Biblical religion, however, has 'de-godded' the pagan pantheons, and thus drastically reduced the available witnesses! So, heaven, earth, mountains – and stones – have to do (cf. Isa. 1:2; Mic. 6:2).

We are warming to the wonder, however, when we note the significant place where this covenant renewal occurred – at Shechem (v. 25); more precisely, at 'the sanctuary of Yahweh' in Shechem (v. 26). We can't help it. Our minds go back to Genesis 12:6-7. It was here at Shechem that Yahweh promised Abram, 'To your seed I will give this land' (Gen. 12:7).[18]

---

themselves wholly to the Lord. There is no need, therefore, of serious examination, lest we be carried aloft by some giddy movement, and so fail of success in our very first attempts.'

[15] English versions usually translate with the colourless 'made a covenant', obscuring the sacrificial allusion in the Hebrew verb *karat* (to cut, i.e. animals). For the background on 'cutting a covenant', see *TDOT*, 2:262-64 (Weinfield); *TWOT*, 1:457; and *ISBE*, rev. ed., 1:790-91 (Thompson); for its biblical-theological import, see especially O. Palmer Robertson, *The Christ of the Covenants* (Phillipsburg, N.J.: Presbyterian and Reformed, 1980), 7-15.

[16] See further Meredith G. Kline, *Treaty of the Great King* (Grand Rapids: Eerdmans, 1963), 13-26.

[17] Woudstra (*Joshua*, 358) rightly points out the emphasis falls on what Yahweh had spoken, not on what the people had said. Thus the '*grace*-shuss' acts of Yahweh (vv. 2-13) will function as an accusing witness should Israel prove faithless. Incidentally, Joshua's 'this stone will be a witness against us' is no sign he was suffering from a primitive animistic hangover – no more than was Jesus when he said, 'This cup is the new covenant.' We shouldn't even be very disturbed about Joshua's stone hearing. No one gets upset when we state, 'This book says....' People who believe in speaking books should tolerate those who prefer hearing stones.

[18] The translation reflects the emphatic position of 'to your seed' in the Hebrew text – particularly strange, since Abram at that time had no seed, in fact, couldn't (Gen. 11:30).

Now, 600 years (plus or minus) later, here is Abraham's seed at Promise Place – Shechem – having the land – no falling words.[19]

But the real wonder of covenant religion is that there is any covenant at all. For Joshua to take the lead in renewing the covenant (as, apparently, in our chapter) means that there must be a covenant to renew. But whoever heard of a covenant-making God (cf. Exod. 34:10)?

> The ideas of a covenant between a deity and a people is unknown to us from other religions and cultures…. It seems, however, that the covenantal idea was a special feature of the religion of Israel, the only one to demand exclusive loyalty and to preclude the possibility of dual or multiple loyalties such as were permitted in other religions, where the believer was bound in diverse relationships to many gods. The stipulation in political treaties demanding exclusive fealty to one king corresponds strikingly with the religious belief in one single, exclusive deity.[20]

Hence there were treaties and covenants in the ancient world. Covenants between kings and vassals, covenants between equals. But where can we find a covenant God, a God who, as Alec Motyer puts it, 'makes and keeps promises'? Where do we hear of a God who binds himself by covenant to a people? Where is there such an unusual God? Only in Israel. Your knees should bend and worship begin: 'Who is a God like you…?' (Mic. 7:18; 1 Kings 8:23).

Study Questions:

1. Why was it necessary for Joshua to recount and review God's grace-filled history of Israel?

---

[19] Neither can we help our minds going back to Genesis 35:4. It was at Shechem that Jacob called his family to 'put away the foreign gods that are among you' (Gen. 35:2); then 'Jacob buried them under the oak at Shechem' (35:4, NIV). Now, hundreds of years later, the demand is the same (Josh. 24:23). And Jacob's family must obey it. Hence Shechem proclaims the comfort of Yaweh's fidelity and issues a call for Israel's.

[20] Moshe Weinfield, 'Berith', *TDOT*, 2:278. See also Robertson, *The Christ of the Covenants*, p. 4 n.2.

2. Do you find the mysteries of God – the darkness you sometimes endure – difficult to accept?

3. Does God's honesty of showing the hard along with the easy, encourage you?

4. In what ways does God continue to display his power toward the church? Does this make you more dependent upon him?

5. Have you taken a look in the rear view mirror to see how God has protected you? Does it cause you to worship him or ask why it happened that way?

6. How has God's provision for you been both necessary and abundant?

7. The commitment which Joshua calls for is both large and deep. Does Christ demand such commitment from his followers?

8. Are you humbled or rise in praise when you realize and believe that the God of creation really wants to have a relationship with you? (It should!)

Subject Index

Scripture Index

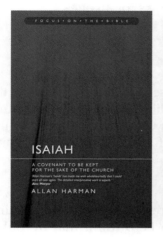

Christian Focus Publications
publishes books for all ages

Our mission statement –

STAYING FAITHFUL
In dependence upon God we seek to impact the world through literature faithful to His infallible Word, the Bible. Our aim is to ensure that the Lord Jesus Christ is presented as the only hope to obtain forgiveness of sin, live a useful life and look forward to heaven with Him.

REACHING OUT
Christ's last command requires us to reach out to our world with His gospel. We seek to help fulfill that by publishing books that point people towards Jesus and help them develop a Christ-like maturity. We aim to equip all levels of readers for life, work, ministry and mission.

Books in our adult range are published in three imprints.

Christian Focus contains popular works including biographies, commentaries, basic doctrine and Christian living. Our children's books are also published in this imprint.

Mentor focuses on books written at a level suitable for Bible College and seminary students, pastors, and other serious readers. The imprint includes commentaries, doctrinal studies, examination of current issues and church history.

Christian Heritage contains classic writings from the past.

Christian Focus Publications, Ltd
Geanies House, Fearn,
Ross-shire, IV20 1TW, Scotland, United Kingdom
info@christianfocus.com

For details of our titles visit us on our website
www.christianfocus.com